SIAMESE BESTIARY

SIAMESE BESTIARY

Written & illustrated by
KRISTIAAN INWOOD

WILDWOOD HOUSE LONDON
BOOKWISE (AUSTRALIA)

Certain material in this book previously appeared,
in somewhat different form,
in 'The Asia Magazine' and 'Sawasdee' magazine.

First published in Great Britain 1979

Wildwood House Ltd
1 Prince of Wales Passage
117 Hampstead Road
London NW1 3EE

Book Wise (Australia) Pty Ltd
104 Sussex Street
Sydney 2000

ISBN Paperback 0 7045 0368 9

Typeset by the
Craftsman Press, Bangkok.
Printed and bound by
Biddles Ltd, Guildford,
Great Britain.

For Anong,
'A' 'B' & 'C'

Introduction

Thailand. Neglected, overgrown, fertile orchards. Thousands of trees. An infinitely rich tropical confectionery of yellows and greens. Some trees recognisable. Some not. Among others, mango, flame, jackfruit, rose apple, papaya, guava, pomelo, durian, orange, gigantic banana trees and towering coconut palms jostle for breathing space. Dense undergrowth spreads between them like rising flood waters. The air is clean, fresh, perfumed with pollen and blossom, and most sounds are natural – wind-rustled leaves, chirping insects, birds clearing their throats, lizards vociferously complaining and sometimes, some evenings, somewhere, unseen, someone wistfully plays a bamboo flute. Were it not for a thin overhead spaghetti of telephone wires and electric cables threading through trees and following an intricate maze of narrow, twisting dirt paths, it would be easy to forget that traffic jams, lung-clogging diesel fumes and the frenetic clamour and passion of commerce are but ten short minutes away.

An old wooden house stands in the middle of the orchards. Trees crowd against a balcony girdling three sides of the house to bring insect chatter and birdsong through open windows. A dirt track drops from a road two hundred yards away, twists through overgrown trees, around a few scattered houses and many shallow ponds, like a frenzied snake, and abruptly stops a few yards beyond the house's front gate. Perpetually widened by trampling feet and wooden oxcart wheels, the original footpath either avoided long-removed obstacles – a stream, large trees, houses – or was blazed by a capricious drunk.

In dry weather the house is delightful. The house is all windows. Entire walls can be opened out to let the outside world in. In every room breezes relayed from the trees circulate luxuriously. Even black footprints on walls and ceilings – the builders were a motley bunch – seem not incongruous as sunlight streams inside to illuminate dust particles levitating towards the roof. Butterflies, birds and insects enter through glassless windows and flutter nervously in search of exits.

During the rainy season the house is a sieve. Rain, vertical, diagonal, horizontal, smashes against the house, penetrates shuttered windows and gaps beneath the roof, and sometimes cascades down inside walls as the building trembles and shakes from vibrations made by wood-burning locomotives on a branch line a quarter of a mile away. If it rains *too* much (whatever that means) catfish in streams and ponds surrounding the house quietly walk away. The track rapidly becomes a bog, impassable except by trekking ankle deep through rich oriental toffee.

The journey is made even more undesirable (nightmarish) by the not unreasonable fear of encountering snakes as they seek higher ground. At night the unlit track – forget about moonlight and lightning flashes – offers horrendous possibilities. Snakes are nocturnal creatures. They *hunt* at night. In rain? Each rustle in undergrowth bordering the track is a starving, half-maddened king cobra *lusting* for food, or a python, or a banded krait; sweet Jesus, even a sighted earthworm would stop the heart. *Hah, nothing to be afraid of. Snakes are more frightened of humans than humans are of snakes.* Nonsense. Rubbish. Impossible. Especially for this human. A hermit impulse (fear) ensures ensconcement inside a dwelling resembling the interior of a defrosting refrigerator. Water drips, drips, drips on to the floor, stains expand on the walls and, outside, frogs croak excessively m-o-n-o-t-o-u-s monologues.

One particular occasion: draining the nth beer bottle in the damp, shuttered tomb, a decision born of claustrophobia – to the balcony. Glass and bottles in hand, upstairs. Outside, it is cool, black, wet. Palm trees are vague silhouettes against a starless sky. A soft drizzle washes the night. Still the the frogs croak. An hour of beery meditation – this 'n' that, boozy fantasies, comfortable reveries, the articulate wish that mosquitos could be persuaded to practise contraception. A fuddled mind demands sleep.

Flop down on the bed, ignore a sub-culture of insects sharing an unsprayed room, succumb to sleep. One last conscious thought. Damn the frogs! Can't they make any other sound?

Come morning the sun is shining. Children's laughter comes from the distance and birds sing full-throated choruses. Walk around the balcony and savour fresh air. Seen through the trees, the few distant neighbours are like ideal Victorian children – seen but rarely heard. The outside world is *somewhere* out there. The trees have been brightly varnished by the rain. A thousand different greens strike the eye. Palm fronds dissect the sky into countless blue slivers; freighted with coconuts, lower branches sag.

Bathe. Breakfast. Downstairs, water in the bathroom is ridiculously cold. Grit teeth, shiver, grunt, hawk, spit, wash, scrub, rinse, dry body and go straight to the refrigerator. House lizards on top of the door scoot away. Open the door. Mother Hubbard emptiness, ah wait, one ice-encrusted bottle of beer, frosted vegetables – nothing else. Confronted with such a choice, open the bottle, pour, drink, ruminate. Alone in the house, sharing it with assorted wildlife, wishing wife were here.

Wife, non-English speaking daughter of a Thai farmer with hundreds of wives, thousands of children and millions of relatives, is in hospital. Nothing serious. Unless having a baby, our first, *is* serious. Something to discover in the months and years ahead. During the pregnancy, from every quarter, the inevitable question, 'What do you want?' Only half-facetiously, the invariable answer, 'A gibbon.' Having perused Darwin's *Origin of Species* and numerous other volumes on genes, chromosomes and related motherjazz, realised the possibility was remote. But half-hoped. After all, father a freak and the world gasps. Royalties from books, articles, lectures, television appearances, advertising . . . yes, an early retirement. Now wifeless and drinking beer for breakfast. A half-complaint. Feeling disorientated

and wishing days will pass quickly before wife and son, both beautiful in my eyes, return.

More half-pickled meditations interrupted by watching a platoon of ants forage among debris in the sink. Silently grateful to have been spared the trouble of educating and house-training a gibbon. Watching a spider dance to the edge of the table when WHAM BANG HOT DAMN an idea. A book.

Specifically, a book about insects and animals in and around the house. The house is virtually a private zoo, a retreat for various itinerants, and, for numerous reasons, means a lot to me. A love affair, marriage and now the birth of my first son; many hours spent watching and drawing temporary inmates – snakes, lizards, frogs, spiders, birds, turtles, etc.; and . . . well, many pleasant memories nestle against my innermost heart.

The idea takes hold. Drain the glass, dress, lock the house and speed to the hospital. Walk swiftly through dark corridors, encounter nostril-twitching odours of the maternity wards, an air-conditioned honeycomb smelling of refrigerated disinfectant and urine, until reaching the top room where wife and child are staying.

Wife, Anong, looking radiant. Son, Hilary, bright pink, screwing up his eyes against a bright outside world only three mornings old. Take him in my arms and talk with Anong. As Anong and self gabble happy nonsense about everything and nothing, Hilary urinates into my breast pocket. The book is baptised, blessed, fertilised, christened and launched.

This is it.

The first week Anong and Hilary are home is an eventful one. Thai friends scattered throughout the orchards regularly visit. They bring presents like talcum powder, towels, fruit – and bottles of local rice whisky to be drunk immediately. Everyone wishes to inspect the son of this very popular Thai girl. Verdicts are uniformly favourable. Alcoholic consumption equals if not exceeds that of the rest of the year. By the end of the week Hilary has a year's supply of talcum powder, we are ankle-deep in fruit, bottles, tins of powdered milk, towels and napkins, and I'm feeling a sprightly sixty-five.

The first Sunday morning, to satisfy Anong's feelings and to make 'merit' for Hilary, we feed Buddhist monks from a nearby monastery. Carrying umbrellas to protect their shaved skulls from the fierce sun, the monks thread single-file through the orchards, bright orange robes singing against sunlit yellows and greens. Friends, neighbours and people I've never seen before help prepare and serve mountains of food. As soon as the monks depart, bellies full and bearing small gifts, bottles miraculously appear. Enough food remains to feed a battalion of exhausted paratroopers. Women and men segregate into two groups and sit on the floor to eat. Children scamper, whistle and hoot throughout the house. Early evening, every adult male is pleasantly stoned.

One morning, bureaucratic regulations demand that Anong make the pilgrimage to the local district office to register Hilary's birth, leaving me alone with my sleeping son. Naturally enough, Hilary wakes five minutes after Anong leaves and starts howling his head off. Coax, soothe, embrace, cradle, croon, desperately try to insert a milk bottle between his gaping jaws. No luck. Incredible screams. Fantastic lungs. Anyone passing outside would think I am trying to strangle him. His vocal chords are well-developed if nothing else.

After five minutes I am panicking. Short of asphyxiation, I can think of no way of silencing him. His angry litany of howl, howl, howl becomes punctuated with hiccups. Cradling him with both arms, I walk outside. An itinerant noodle vendor advises me to make him drink water. This, she assures me, will stop him burping. I thank her and return inside.

Somehow (the exact method is still classified information), I insert the teat of a water bottle between his lips. Gurgle. Gurgle. Gurgle. Half a bottle. He thrusts the bottle away. Hiccup. Hiccup. Hiccup. Ye gods.

Replace him in his cot. Pace up and down against a background noise of steady burps. Now what to do? Shock! Of course!! The classic solution!!! Lean over his cot, growl and make a Frankenstein leer. Hiccup-howl-hiccup. Limbs working overtime, fists angrily clenched, mouth agape, Hilary emits one continual hiccuped howling scream.

Terrified, scoop him up and run to our nearest neighbour. Break several Olympic records. The neighbour is dress-making, sees me weaving through the trees like a berserk guerilla and stands up in alarm. I thrust the burping Hilary into her arms, take several deep breaths and coherently explain the problem.

She hoists Hilary on to her shoulder, pats his back and softly croons. Silence. A knowing smile. Unbelievable. The little lecher. Nothing like a woman's arms.

Profuse thanks. Take him away. Little fellow's eyes are heavy. Tiptoe back to the house. Gently replace him in his cot. A breath-holding retreat to a chair. Quiet.

A minute later, howl, howl, howl. Rapid inspection. He can't sleep because his napkin is flooded. A five-minute change. The longest five minutes I have ever known. Repeatedly stab myself with safety pins, pickle him in powder, blood and sweat, constantly curse, and dispose of soiled linen. Talk about on-the-job training. Slump back into the chair.

No rest, however. By now Hilary is wide awake and demands even more attention. Milk. Mix, stir, shake, wish I had a cow, insert bottle into his mouth. Chuckle, gurgle. Replace him into his cot but he refuses to drink the stuff unless he's held. Stand holding him and bottle.

A sudden wind sends things toppling from shelves. Window shutters slam. Trees are bending sideways. Leaves blow through the house. It gets very dark. The sun has been blotted out. Wind is coming from every direction. A sudden tropical downpour threatens. Insert Hilary into his cot. He howls. Pick him up again. A relentless sucking silence.

A sudden whoosh and rain sweeps into the house horizontally. Shelter Hilary from the rain and frantically begin shutting windows. It seems like someone has pulled the plug. The floor, his cot are rapidly drenched. Race upstairs, Hilary, unperturbed, in my arms, slamming windows (and fingers) shut one-handed. The balcony is flooded. Paintings are soaked. Our bed is a damp, springy mess.

Finally shut every window. Drenched in perspiration and rainwater. Hilary contentedly sucking in milk and clenching and unclenching his fists. Dry him and self with a towel. Further streak him with blood from window shutting. Rainwater cascades from the roof. Seen through the front door, trees are a twisting, battered, opaque grey mass.

Hilary withdraws his mouth from the bottle, gently burps and sleeps peacefully. Within two minutes the rain stops. The sun reappears. The house heats up like an oven. Search for somewhere to put Hilary. Cot, table, floor and chairs are soaked. I wrap him in a dry towel and place him in the only dry place I can find. Open the windows again. Pools of water everywhere.

Not sure if I have any talent for telepathy but sure as hell am trying. *Anong, get back quick!* The kitchen, windows still open, is flooded. Outside, washing hangs dripping limp on the line. Walk outside to look at the sky. Difficult to believe. Everywhere is blue.

Return inside and belly-crawl under the table to retrieve fallen objects. A saronged pair of legs move into vision. Anong reappears.

'Where's Hilary?'

'In the sink.'

'What?'

'He's in the sink'

'What's he doing there? The poor child!'

The 'poor child' is fast asleep.

'Look at his cot! The floor!! The walls!!! What have you been *doing?*'

'What have *I* been doing?'

'Don't shout! Now you've woken him up. Poor child.'

Gurgle. Chuckle. Chuckle. She moves to pick him up.

She looks at him and gasps. 'He's covered in blood!'

'It's mine, not his, don't worry.'

'Couldn't you have bled elsewhere? Look at that! What happened to the kitchen? It's flooded!'

'It rained!'

'Couldn't you have closed the windows? What a mess!'

'Wait till you see upstairs.'

'What?'

'Never mind.'

'Did you take the washing in?'

'No'

Hilary whimpers, buries his face in Anong's breasts. The little glutton. She sits on the wet floor in front of me, lifts her blouse and pops a nipple into his mouth. Peace.

'I can't believe it! I leave you alone for twenty minutes and this is what happens!'

Teeth-gnashing, purple-faced, impotent rage. Never get angry when you're on your stomach. 'Have you registered him yet?'

'No. I forgot the house registration. I'll just get it and go back.'

'Uh-huh.'

'What do you mean, uh-huh?'

'I'll go. *You* stay here.'

'This morning you *demanded* I go.'

'That was this morning.'

'What's made you change your mind so quickly?'

'The fact that I'm not equipped to be left alone with a twelve-day-old child.'

'What are you talking about?'

'Those,' pointing. 'I haven't got any boobs!'

Roles were clearly defined thereafter.

A few weeks after Hilary's birth, one of Anong's elder sisters visited us. A plump, merry widow, Muang sprang an emotional *coup d'etat* on the neighbourhood during her nine-day stay. Not least of her charms was her speech. She spoke an almost incomprehensible (to me) dialect of Thai, a pink, personal language filtered through teeth stained scarlet by incessant betel-nut chewing.

Her first remark when she arrived was typical. Anong has dark brown skin. Hilary is white, the colour of an Englishman who has avoided sunlight as though it were the black plague. When Muang first saw him she looked at Anong, examined Hilary, sagaciously nodded and looked at Anong.

'Sister,' she said seriously, 'you are a buffalo.'

'Eh?'

'Buffaloes are dark and have light-skinned babies.'

'Mmmm. Did you have a pleasant journey. . .?'

During her stay Muang occupied herself by cradling Hilary, gossiping with Anong in an ear-bending mixture of Thai, Laotian and Chinese, and making *som tam malagor*, a tongue-tingling dish of crab meat, shredded papaya, tomatoes, lemon juice and chillies. Often I would return home to find the kitchen overflowing with neighbourhood women, all eating *som tam malagor*, drinking coconut milk and passing Hilary around to be nursed in turn by each woman. The women would be sweating profusely, sucking in air to cool their tongues – the dish is really hot – and listening to Muang hold forth on a variety of subjects. Whenever Muang held court the kitchen was full.

Buying crabs for her precious *som tam* was not enough of a challenge for Muang. She caught them herself in pools around the house, attractive land crabs, bodies never much larger than a baby's clenched fist.

During Muang's stay I was making drawings of crabs, none of which were good. Every evening she inspected the drawings and once brought me a plastic bowl containing two crabs to be used as models. That same evening she decided to impart her knowledge of crab-lore, about which it appeared, she knew a lot. Our communication was terrible. Neither understood the other's use of Thai so that Anong, when she could stop laughing, had to interpret our respective comments to each other.

One of the crabs kept circling sideways inside the bowl and looked extremely aggressive. I asked Muang why. Her answer was something about crabs having to move sideways because they have too many damn feet and only trip themselves up if they walk forwards.

Crab anatomy was no puzzle to Muang. She said that crab claws were once crab legs. She maintained that because crabs have difficulty walking with so many legs a particularly sensible crab once held his front legs up together before him to make walking easier. Others followed his example. Before long, front legs evolved into claws. Therefore, Muang believed, it is only a matter of time before crabs do the same with other legs. Eventually they will have no legs, just claws. They will be born cripples and be 'really damned easy to catch'.

Her nine days passed far too quickly. Everyone was sorry to see Muang return to her country home except, perhaps, neighbourhood crabs. The crab population had taken a fearful bashing.

The crab drawing here is for Muang.

The longer I stay here the more difficult it becomes to imagine a Thailand without the ubiquitous, tiny house-lizards locally known as *chinchoks* (Gekkonidae). It is relatively easy to imagine an England without fish 'n' chips; and Italy without spaghetti; or even an India without cows. But a Thailand without chinchoks? No way. Unthinkable.

Once, Anong and I spent a lazy five days at a friend's beachside bungalow. The setting was idyllic enough to make travel agents drool – a broad, palm-fringed bay with clear water and clean white sand as soft as talcum powder. Dwarfed among the palms, the bungalow was separated by hundreds of trees from the nearest people who lived in a small fishing village a mile away. The bay was so remote that during our stay the only footprints on the beach were ours. Indeed, the only other person we ever saw was a lone fisherman who would wade through the shallows every evening, periodically casting his net to catch small fish.

In contrast to the overpowering beauty of our surroundings, the bungalow was vaguely oppressive. The vibrations weren't quite right. We both felt mildly ill-at-ease but couldn't define exactly what was wrong. It didn't matter too much since we spent most of our stay outdoors.

On the last afternoon, however, torrential rain forced us to stay inside the bungalow. We were both sprawled on the bed. I was half dozing, half-listening to the rain when Anong suddenly sat up and slapped my knee.

'Chinchoks!'

'Eh? Whassamatter?'

'There aren't any chinchoks!'

'What are you talking about? There are no chinchoks *where*?'

'Here. Where else?'

'Oh, there must be!'

'Can you see any?'

'No, but they must be somewhere.'

'Huh,' she snorted, pulling me off the bed. 'Let's look.'

We spent the next fifteen minutes searching the bungalow for chinchoks. The KGB couldn't have made a more thorough search. We couldn't find a single one. It was a bit eerie. No friendly house-lizards! Why not? Our collective imagination ran amok. Something was terribly, ominously wrong. Creaking shutters, an abrupt breeze that lifted curtains to the ceiling, and a wind-slammed door suddenly seemed meaningful. Had either of us been alone and discovered there were no chinchoks, we would have fled the place immediately. No chinchoks, ferchrissakes! We were very happy to leave the next morning.

Without chinchoks, houses (hotels, restaurants, gambling dens, shops, palaces, warehouses, bars, massage parlours, gaols, garages, temples, hospitals, brothels, museums, morgues and, dammit, beachside bungalows)

seem incomplete — once I counted seventeen covering my studio ceiling and walls. And without them another form of cheap entertainment would be lost. A chinchok stalks a butterfly, inching forward, belly-crawling like a Sioux scout in a vintage western, avoiding rocks, seeking the sparse shelter of small bushes, snaking through short grass, distant tomtoms throb, an owl hoots, camp lights flicker. The final few inches are covered in a sudden, vicious sprint — a near miss, the tomtoms stop, a blink and another hunt.

With rare exceptions, chinchoks are extraordinarily playful, transforming walls and ceilings into nurseries, effortlessly defying gravity thanks to suction pads on their feet. If Isaac Newton had ever seen a Thai chinchok. . . .

The lizard population in and about the house has to be seen to be believed. Many, many shapes, sizes and colours. Sometimes there seem to be at least as many different lizards as there are matchbox labels.

Least attractive of them all are the chinchok's large cousins, the *tokays.* Irascible, as graceless as rampaging pigs, they eat whatever they come across — insects by the kilo, young birds, chinchoks, snakes (reportedly), young tokays, anything edible will do. Beady-eyed, unattractive, fearless, they clump all over the house (my house, at least), patrol the roof, gobble prey under the eaves and terrorize everything and everyone. (Long-time residents probably have their favourite recollections of when they were most scared here. 'Face to face with a king cobra' or '. . .collision with a ten-wheel truck.' Mine concerns just having completed a freezingly cold and candlelit shower one winter night during a power cut and lifting a towel off the rack to uncover a maliciously grinning tokay.)

Don't like them one little bit. Chinchoks are far nicer. Despite superficial similarities, differences between the two creatures are many. Long, dark nights are punctuated by the chinchok's whispered squeak chuckles; the tokay emits a harsh, eerie, onomatopoeic *to-kaaay.* Chinchoks are always playing; tokays *never* play. Chinchoks lose their tails and look cute; tokays lose their tails and look even more sinister. Tokays are megalomaniacs; chinchoks dig Sesshu, Bach, John D. MacDonald, Miles Davis and Zen Buddhism. The list is endless.

Even more intimidating than the tokay is a smooth, black-and-grey lizard that looks like a snake with legs. He enters the house frequently and frightens everyone. Very fast. Anong and I have made several attempts to capture him — we have even tried to lasso him — but have never had any success. At one time his capture seemed of paramount importance. We discussed and rejected several schemes. Probably the most practical of our plans, we believed that, using the *Kama Sutra* as a manual, we would train a chinchok to seduce him. When his attention was distracted we would grab him. Brilliant, we thought. But nothing ever came of it because the chinchok refused to learn Sanskrit.

Dragonflies congregate before sunset over a pond beside the house. They employ their own power in short bursts to fractionally miss palm fronds before drifting into circular flight patterns. At regular intervals soloists swoop down, skim dark waters and accelerate to return above trees from where recurrent flight patterns begin. Effortlessly the eye follows their carefree flights around palm fronds exulting and curtseying from breeze-swept branches. Upwards of thirty bodies are blackened against the rich blue of an evening sky.

Daily, a lone dragonfly enters the studio, whirs into paintings, collides with the frosted glass of the south wall and continually tries to break through the seductive brightness upon which chinchoks crouch in ambush. Rarely is the dragonfly caught but neither is it given much peace. Come twilight it discerns the relative lightness of windows and doors and, after initially clumsy attempts, makes good its exit. Upwards, upwards it flies, unleashed from the confines of the room, upwards, upwards high above tree tops and out of sight. The following day another suffers the same confinement.

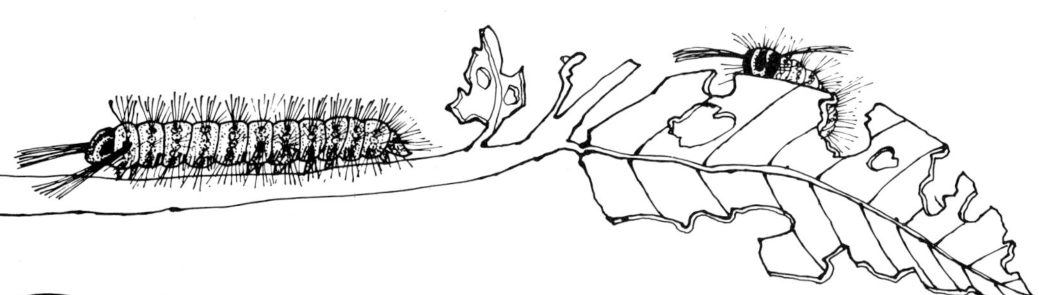

Crunch. Crunch. Crunch. The lower leaves of a rose apple tree behind the house are systematically eaten by hundreds of caterpillars relentlessly chewing their way upwards. Birds pick them off without making any apparent impact on their numbers. Crunch. Crunch. Crunch. Chlorophyll-green hairies nibble slow advances. Crunch. Crunch. Crunch. Turn over, segments undulating – you know it, not hear it – with a squashy sound as siphoned leaves become a spinach-green mess inflating their bodies. Wonder, they never seem to grow. Crunch. Crunch. Crunch. The tree appears to be doing a strip-tease. Lower limbs are denuded first. Crunch. Crunch. Crunch.

Pick a caterpillar. It curls in the palm of the hand. Ah, it has intelligence to stop. Oh, oh, spoken too soon. Uncurl, ripple with energy, move down to finger tips. No way out. Over and upside down along the back of the hand. Jaws masticate air. Can't stop. Crunch. Crunch. Crunch. O.K. We're all equally well-programmed.

Feasted on by birds, snatched by other enemies including ham-fisted children, the survivors change into butterflies (beautiful butterflies), the sight of which gladdens the heart. Perhaps even that denuded tree feels its sacrifice worthwhile even though the beauty of butterflies can't disguise one important and sadly accurate fact. Butterflies have suicidal tendencies.

During the day, every day, hot, rainy and cool seasons, butterflies join the lone dragonfly on the glass of the studio's south wall and make easy meals for chinchoks. Incapable of retreat, they collide with the glass – brightest surface in the room – and continually thrash themselves in futile efforts to leave the room by passing *through* the glass. They simply will not retreat. Chinchoks feast, a wing wafer here, a wing flake there before grabbing the head and body and wings and scurrying away to devour the wing-flapping nuts in peace.

Once a particularly beautiful specimen with a wing span as wide as a hand's length flew in. It followed exactly the same procedure, beating itself against the glass and not retreating. Sigh. Pity. I capture it, walk on to the balcony and release it. Two minutes later the same butterfly is in the same place on the same glass. Pity and exasperation. Chinchoks dart and a wing is half chewed. A chinchok scowls as the butterfly is plucked from its nose. On to the balcony again to release it once more. Within a minute the idiot returns. I give up and watch. Two chinchoks strike, one severs the head, looks astonished as the decapitated body drops, wings beating, down to the bottom of a painting, flap, flap, flap on the floor. It chases off the other chinchok, falls down the window screen and slides down a wet painting. Holy Lizard, is this believable? Wings without a

head, flap, flap, flap. It hesitates, grabs the wings and tastes linseed oil. Its mouth is too small. It can't possibly eat it. It chokes, coughs and retreats. The second chinchok races in and tears one wing away – looking like a glutton trying to swallow a bowlful of noodles in one gulp. I resolve never to interfere again.

Hilary is cradled by Anong. A butterfly lands on his soft pate. He chuckles. His hands rise without co-ordination and the butterfly soars away. Hilary screams his frustration, lower lip angrily protruding. A tearless cry. Butterfly, thing, come back. We try to soothe and coax him with other attractions. His heart is set on a butterfly. I begin to lose my mind. I walk outside and hunt around trees and bushes. Eventually I capture another butterfly and return inside to show my angry son. A huge grin creases his face. Chuckle. Chuckle. I can't hold the butterfly for ever so I release it. Anger. Hilary loses his temper, Anong loses her temper. Tantrums and absolute freaking chaos. Inevitably, that universal pacifier – expose a nipple for breast-fed contentment. Another habit germinates. (Wish I could have similar treatment every time I get upset, angry or discouraged.)

Outside, butterfly villains hover over bushes and flowers like flamboyant bees. Nice. But never get involved.

One night, during a violent thunderstorm, we heard dogs growling and something knocking bang, bang, bang against the front gate After ignoring and quietly cursing the persistent noise for half an hour – a clumsy burglar, a canine gang bang, we couldn't have cared less, we didn't want to get wet – we opened the front door. Two dogs, saturated by rain and a stream of water cascading from a tin roof, were pushing a rocklike object against the gate. The dogs were cautiously pushing it with their paws, retreating, gaining courage to sniff the sodden wet object, paw it and retreat again. Bangs, flashbulb pops of lightning and windswept rain. We looked closer and saw a glistening shell belonging to either a tortoise or a turtle.

Anong shooed the dogs away, dashed outside to pick up the shell and ran back inside, soaked. She spread a dry newspaper on the floor and placed the shell on top. We sat on the floor watching the shell, wondering if the creature was dead or alive. A head slowly appeared. The creature noticed us and quickly withdrew. Several times the head slowly appeared and was quickly withdrawn. Eventually, after about ten minutes, the creature fully extended its head and surveyed the room.

A tortoise or a turtle. We weren't sure. I'd seen films of turtles laying ping pong balls on a Malaysian beach but couldn't tell what this was. We half filled a washing bowl with water – not full to avoid drowning it – sprinkled lettuce leaves inside and inserted the creature. Then we waited to see what would happen. We figured that if it didn't like water it would have to be a tortoise; or a turtle that couldn't swim. And if it did like water, then it would have to be a turtle; or an amphibious tortoise.

The creature passively sank to its neck, ignored the leaves and remained motionless.

'Why doesn't it move?'

'Maybe it's embarrassed.'

'Animals don't feel embarrassment. Only humans do.'

'That's not true. We had a goat at home that wouldn't relieve itself when people were around.'

It was late so we went upstairs leaving *it* alone in darkness.

The following morning we found he or she in the same position although many of the leaves had disappeared. Later, a hawker identified our guest as a turtle. The rain had long since stopped so Anong took the turtle to a large lotus-filled pond beside the main road. She placed it in the water and away it swam. Thereafter, each time we passed the pond, we found ourselves looking for a sight of 'our turtle'.

We never saw it again. Soon after, the pond was filled in preparation for widening the main road.

At the mention of snakes, my neck muscles stiffen. At the sight of snakes, physiological hell breaks loose. But, schizophrenically, I invariably go first to the reptile house during zoo visits to spend a masochistic hour watching the snakes.

Not that I need bother. In the house and environs Anong and I have either seen or stumbled across 'harmless' green tree snakes camouflaged among foliage; cobras, really frightening, spread hoods, the entire belligerent routine; six-foot-long diamond-patterned horrors moving through undergrowth; a black-and-green snake opening its jaws unbelievably wide to swallow a tree lizard; pit vipers with triangular green heads and red-tipped tails; brown water snakes; curious black bootlaces wriggling across the verandah; and other anonymous horrors about which we remain hopelessly ignorant.

Early one morning, Anong was hanging out washing behind the house. She felt movement on the hem of her sarong, looked down and saw a small snake. She killed it. With admirable *sangfroid* she continued to peg clothes to the line. She felt another movement and looked down again. Another snake was clubbed to death. She fled into the house and ran upstairs to see me. I was finishing a drawing of a snake striking at a rat. Jellylike, she flopped to the floor.

'I've just killed a snake.'

'Oh, God. Is it dead?'

'Of course it's dead. I said I killed it.'

'Where?'

'Behind the kitchen. In fact, I killed two.'

'Oh, no. Were they the same?'

'Brother and sister.'

'Oh, no.'

Move into a tenth-floor apartment. Buy a mongoose. Better, buy a dozen. Emigrate to Ireland. Or New Zealand. Advertise for a suit of armour. Walk on stilts. . . Thoughts evaporate and a fragmented mind retunes to snakes outside the kitchen . . . my kitchen . . . the drawing loses something.

'What are you drawing?'

'I think you'd better see for yourself.'

'Why?'

'Just see for yourself.'

'Ah! It's a . . . oh . . .'

'Don't say that. It's not polite.'

Anong encounters snakes more frequently than anyone should. Once, eight months pregnant with Hilary, she unfastened a sun blind on the balcony. Her scream sent me running outside, just in time to see a green-yellow-and-black snake slither over the balcony and disappear down the outside wall. I ran downstairs to check if it had entered the house through the open windows. It had vanished without trace.

An earlier encounter with a snake was more painful. We were both in the kitchen one evening. Anong was cooking dinner and I was drawing a spider, sentry in her web.

Our kitchen has every appearance of being an afterthought. It doesn't fit with the rest of the house. Three steps below the level of the dining and living rooms, it has a solid concrete floor and is full of recesses, nooks and crannies. At night, no matter how bright the illumination, a third of the kitchen is filled with dramatic shadow. Squeezed into one of its seven corners is a native-style bathroom, *John 2,* and the back door, both of which remain in semi-darkness.

On this occasion, for some reason I glanced towards the back door and saw a yard-long snake entering the kitchen through a water outflow in the door base. On seeing the snake, Anong snatched up a ten-foot-long strip of picture framing and began using it as a lance, trying to make the snake retreat. I stood directly behind her and shone a torch at the intruder. Instead of retreating, the snake wrapped itself around the framing and began moving towards Anong's hands. Anong panicked, dropped the framing and ran straight into me, knocking me over. As we fell, one of my hands accidentally slapped the light switches and the kitchen plunged into darkness. The torch fell from my other hand and rolled across the floor, stopped under the sink and illuminated a small circle of wall. The only other light came from a charcoal stove which glowed a hellish red.

During the subsequent confusion, Anong and I were as co-ordinated as two monkeys fighting in a sack.

Pain.

'Anong !!!'

'What !!?!'

'Takeyour kneesoffmythroat !!!!'

'Where's the snake?'

'Aaaaaaahhhhhh !!!'

'Have you been bitten!?'

'Iamchokingggg !!'

'What?'

'Getttofffff !!!'

'Let me switch the lights on!'

She did. As I sat up, nursing my neck, we saw the snake retreat through the outflow. We were both indescribably nervous. Appetites vanished and we hurriedly left the kitchen, but not before blocking the hole with a brick. Thereafter, for a matter of months, I refused to go outside

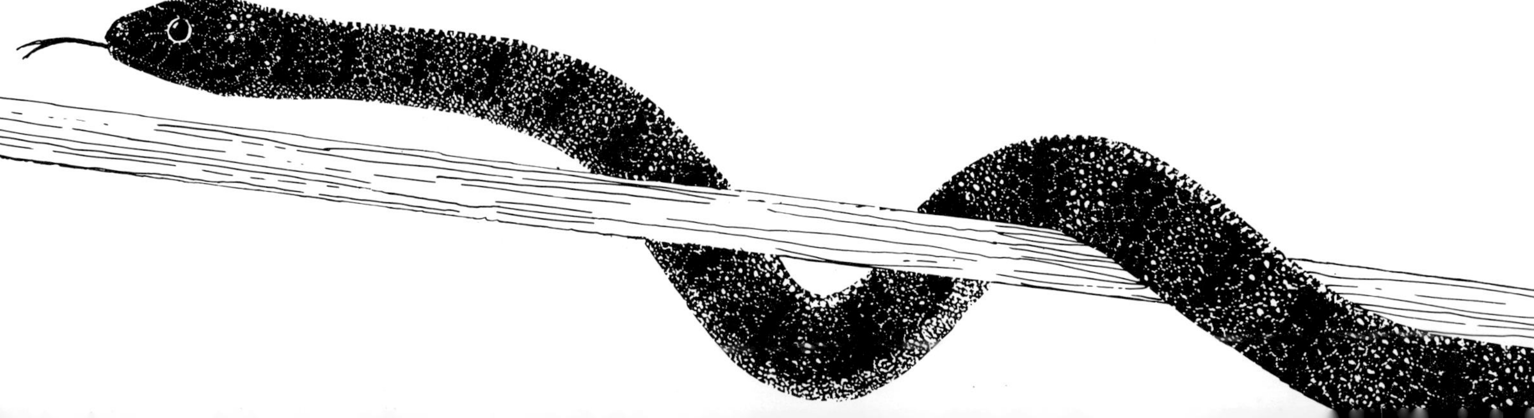

through the back door or use *John 2.* Childhood memories of elders bragging about cobras encountered in toilets in British India were resurrected and became vivid in my mind. Altogether it was a period of great mental anguish, not in the least lessened by Anong's theory that my fear of snakes stemmed from my previous existence when, she was convinced, I must have been a horse.

Not long afterwards, resolving to overcome the more ridiculous aspects of my fear, I decided to visit a one-time farmer turned professional snakecatcher called Kasem, who lives in an isolated house a few miles away where the orchards open into rice fields.

I wanted to ask him how to deal with snakes and was even toying, I repeat, *toying,* with the idea of asking him to teach me how to catch them.

The first time I had met him he gave me some memorable advice about pythons. (Pythons are the most valuable snakes to him – tanned skins from which shoes, belts, wallets or handbags can be made are worth about fifteen US dollars each.) He had been explaining how he catches them.

'What if they can wrap themselves around you?' I had asked.

'You have to squeeze their hearts. Eventually they weaken enough to be manageable.'

'But supposing they are still too strong for you?'

'Then there's only one thing to do.'

'Pray?'

'No,' he grinned, 'bite them. Bite them hard!'

'You're not serious!'

'I am. Bite them and they'll release you immediately.'

'Come on!'

'It's true. I've had to bite them several times and they've always released me immediately. I hate to do it, though. It ruins their skins and makes them almost worthless.'

'Maybe you shouldn't bite so hard.'

Now, when I visit Kasem, he is sitting downstairs in the open space beneath his stilted wooden house. Many huge wooden crates, tightly closed but drilled with air holes, surround him. Each crate contains an assortment of live cobras, pythons, vipers, banded kraits and king cobras, a nightmarish collection with enough venom and muscle to decimate a small village were they ever to escape. Out of sight, the snakes are not out of mind. I can never rid myself of the image of sinewy, muscular forms sluggishly coiling and uncoiling in humid darkness, patiently awaiting opportunities to retaliate against their gaoler.

'Hello, Kasem, has anyone burgled you lately?'

A standing joke. *No one* will ever burgle *his* house. Well, someone might the day all Swiss banks declare themselves bankrupt.

'No,' he smiles, 'but something much worse happened last month.'

'Oh?'

'I was bitten.'

'An occupational hazard,' breezily. 'By what?'

'A king cobra.'

My big mouth. 'Where did that happen?'

'Here, of all places. I had to take one out of its crate to feed it. I was careless because the next thing I knew it was chewing my wrist. I wrenched it off and threw it back into the crate!'

I can 'see' it vividly. Unlike other snakes that strike, bite and withdraw, cobras strike and chew, chew, chew, injecting ever-increasing amounts of venom into the bloodstream.

'The venom sacs were full?'

He nods. 'And how!'

'You used your herbal medicine?'

'Immediately!'

Powdered lemon mushroom and the chopped root of a tree the Thais call 'the mucus of the mongoose', mixed with white whisky or rice wine and immediately swallowed after a snakebite, comprise his herbal medicine.

'And so that worked?'

'No,' ruefully, 'not immediately. Soon I felt so lousy I can hardly describe it.' He pauses in recollection.

'Please try.'

'I couldn't talk properly. I couldn't breathe easily. My eyes were going out of focus. My bones seemed to have melted. I began shivering, yet I was sweating. I felt exhausted and just wanted to sleep. I was certain I was dying. The medicine had always worked before but I was rapidly losing faith in it. As a last desperate measure – I had no choice – I made double the first amount. I couldn't swallow that easily. I half drank, half vomited. Some was expelled through my nose. I started choking but somehow, weak as I was, I forced it down.'

'And that did the trick?'

'Yes, eventually. For hours I didn't feel any worse. I still thought I would die. Then, little by little, I felt slowly better. But it was three days before I felt anything like normal again. Even now my eyes are very sensitive to light and still feel weak.'

'Did you kill the snake afterwards?'

'No. It's still in a crate over there.'

'Have you fed it since?'

'Oh, yes. I'm much more careful now, don't worry.'

Wordlessly, he stands up and walks over to the crates. With extreme delicacy, and no apparent fear, he extracts a black and gold, ten foot, thick-as-my-forearm coil of explosive energy: a truly magnificent king cobra.

Holding it by the tail, Kasem throws the snake, in my direction, to the ground and prods its head away from him with a steel-hooked stick. The snake rears angrily, its eyes eighteen inches above the ground, and spreads its hood.

Looking it in the eye at a distance of six feet is chilling. I am praying Kasem doesn't lose his grip on the creature's tail. If he does, I am dead, herbal medicine or not. Probably the most dangerous snake in the world because of its speed, strength and ferocity, the king cobra deserves total respect. It is utterly fearless and magnificently beautiful. It grows over fifteen feet in length. It is capable of rearing waist-high and outpacing a galloping racehorse. Worshipped by some esoteric Eastern sects, it has long been immortalised in Asian legends. A living nightmare when confronted, it reigns supreme in the forests (on a diet of other snakes) and in hunters' imaginations. Hunters know that should they be unfortunate enough to encounter one deep in the forests, their only real protection is a shotgun blast at point-blank range because surviving the savage attack of a king cobra is about as unlikely as surviving the attentions of a great white shark. An average cobra's venom sacs contain enough poison to kill a thousand rabbits. The king cobra is two, three, four or even five times bigger, longer, stronger, angrier, nastier and meaner than its smaller cousin. Just imagine. . .

With a sudden, frightening burst of speed, the snake arches backwards and attempts to strike at Kasem. Calmly, he manipulates its head with the pole. Slowly, with extreme concentration, he gathers the snake towards him and replaces it in its crate.

'That was the one?'

'That was the one.'

Gulp. . . .

Suffice to say that neither then nor subsequently did I ever burden Kasem with *my* problems regarding snakes.

Many weeks later, lunching at an unusual restaurant where fried-ant omlettes and frog soups are commonplace. Half-way through a peculiar curry, a question forms in my mind: 'Most excellent host, the ingredients of this exotic, oriental curry, tasting of mysterious spices and viands, lovingly prepared during the romantic tropical night by maidens yonder, the ingredients, mine host, are what?'

A blurted question. 'What's this made of?'

'Python,' says he.

The remainder of the meal spent morbidly considering the consequences should the python, oh my God, a freaking python, be reborn in a screaming autistic stomach contracting beneath a blanket of Christalmighty thought. Vulgar speculation becomes ultimately so obscene that I resolve to drink several pints of canal water at the earliest opportunity.

I needn't have worried. That evening when I returned home, still contemplating canal water – and cholera and typhoid and beriberi – the laxative properties of lunch took effect. After a sleepless night I felt that my intestines had never been cleaner, as though I had undergone fifteen intensive years of yogic ablutions. It was a good feeling.

Conclusion: *nothing* gives you a better run for your money than python curry.

In many parts of the world, the night is a time of quiet. Infrequently, the still air is disturbed by the rustling of leaves, the hoot of an owl or the low of cattle: noise and movement are rare. In the tropics, however, nightly insect chatter provides a background rhythm for extensive animal activity.

An ominous buzz betrays the presence of mosquitos bent on nocturnal mischief. Heavy-footed tokays shake window frames in pursuit of prey. Dogs fitfully bark at the passage of human prowlers or snakes. Frogs and crickets produce unvarying songs and moths bruise themselves attempting to enter screened windows. Minute insects circle lights and plummet towards the floor when stunned. Groggily they rise again to orbit like moons around a mother planet.

In dark rooms the loathsome cockroach is foraging, chewing toothbrush bristles in bathrooms and squirting its odious perfume when discovered. Beneath the house gigantic rats are moving warily, ignoring poisoned bait like combat veterans but frequently failing to escape the arrow-swift jaws of a waiting snake. A sudden death chatter is abruptly severed. The hypnotic chorus of insects momentarily halts and then continues. A sudden commotion in a tree and silence. A coconut crashes through leaves of smaller trees and thuds onto the ground like an unexploded bomb. Outside a shuttered kitchen window an emaciated cat scavenges among refuse. Too cowardly, too weak to hunt rats as large as itself, too dull, too slow to catch mice and frogs, the creature miaows in self-pity. Moonlit shadows burden its back with crushing weight. Soon it will die.

Anong and Hilary sleep peacefully and the heart is calm. A walk through the orchards under a black, bejewelled sky. The shapes of palm trees appear even more perfect at night. Scorpions, centipedes and snakes sensed as fellow travellers but no fear. What the eye cannot perceive does not exist. Listening carefully, many different sounds can be distinguished. Cicadae produce their distinctive night song. Water gurgles in a silver-black stream. A series of small splashes counterpoint a frog chorus that suddenly, like a speeded-up record, ends in a geese-like cackle. In a sudden breeze a clump of banana trees stir and nod; and rustle like expensive petticoats. The eye is seduced by a lone firefly erratically moving through the dark leaves of a tree. Like a lazy star it twinkles brightly, dimly, brightly again. The indistinct shapes of bats glide and turn between mango trees, bodies transformed by moonlight into swallows of the dark. The crimson end of a lighted cigarette gives warmth to the cool air. Silvered leaves glisten in motion and palm fronds soothingly nod. A long-tailed lizard darts through the undergrowth. The well-being of leisure among movement envelops the spirit. Everything is soft, magical.

An unhurried return to the dark house.

One sleeps with a quiet joy.

Dear Hilary,

Now that you are five months old and taking a keen delight in your surroundings, let me tell you about ants. Ants are energetic little monomaniacs that never seem to stop working, scavenging, travelling, etc.. Guerilla armies set forth from concealment to hurry to the nearest source of free food. You yourself have seen them as pallbearers for insect corpses. Indeed, you chuckled at the sight, which is the most sensible thing to do. When you grow up you will discover that few people are prepared to laugh at ants. Ants are physically abused and exterminated even when they are no direct threat to anyone. You will see ostensibly sensible people deliberately trample them into the ground for no apparent reason. Interestingly enough, there are many jokes about crows, elephants, camels and other creatures, but few about ants. To the average person ants are not funny. When you are older some people will point out similarities between humans and ants. Beware of such characters. They themselves epitomise the similarities they propound. Quite likely to be ant-tramplers, they will also tell you how ants milk greenfly; how, if they had lungs, ants would rule the world; how ants are able to move something a thousand times their own weight. What they will not tell you is how in ancient times a disgruntled Roman scholar, a congenital ant-hater, perceived the activities of ants as detrimental to an ordered society and coined the then derogatory prefix ant. By the time of Imperial Rome's zenith the word had been expanded to anti. In an unpublished manuscript, Marcus Aurelius theorized that the i was added by Egyptian eunuchs who had lost many of their brethren from pronouncing the

word ant. Supposedly, the prefix ant was particularly difficult for eunuchs to pronounce and a great many had died of suffocation after swallowing their tongues. When, purely by chance, one pronounced the word with an added i and survived, the new pronunciation was swiftly adopted. As every Assyrian schoolboy knew, many new words were coined after the prefix had been standardised. And words came from the most unlikely sources. Old men in the northern deserts of Ethiopia still recount the tale of Sheikh Al Sakambrihar. The sheikh and his caravan were returning home through the great Arabian deserts after a pilgrimage to Mecca. Besides the normal contingent of camels, concubines, counsellors, soldiers and servants, the old man's retinue included a deer. Each evening, before sunset, as camp was made, the sheikh and his closest advisers would sit in a half circle around the deer to admire its physical beauty and sweet disposition. One evening, the sheikh saw an army of ants gather on the deer's back and moved closer to observe them. The advisers also moved closer to see what had attracted their master's attention. They, of course, saw only insects on the animal's quivering back. The old man, however, knew ants when he saw them, having acquired a small English vocabulary from his eldest son who had been educated in Canterbury. With rapt attention he observed two ants separate from the others and creep down the deer's hindquarters. The old man smiled. He remembered the story his son had told him about the verger's daughter and the chorister. 'Ah,' he grunted, 'Ant elope.' The rest is history. Son, I digress. Whatever your feelings about this epistle, I hope that ants will continue to entertain you and that you will be able to avoid sadistically killing them. It is far nicer and far simpler to co-exist with them than to vent your frustrations by obliterating such small creatures. Chuckle on, Hilary,

Libidinous mongrels, some possibly rabid, patrol foothpaths carved through the orchards. Some come from a nearby Buddhist monastery, deposited there when pups or when they had outgrown their use as watchdogs. They form the nucleus of a pack that congregates around houses bordering the orchards to scavenge and fight among themselves when bitches are in season.

Dogs come, dogs go. Some have their cunning aspirations crushed on main roads. Others become rabid, foam at the mouth, bite a few people, turn stupid, fall into canals and drown. Their carcasses float downstream, grey and bloated, and eventually are washed against the banks where they reek in the hot sun. Others disappear or are stolen.

If the dogs share one major characteristic, it must be that a disproportionate number are neurotic. Their standard diet – leftover rice, leftover vegetables, leftover meat scraps – and the incessant heat combine to weaken them and addle their brains. Imagine humans having to find nourishment from equally unsuitable leftovers (dog biscuits, minced horsemeat and jaw-breaking bones) and wearing fur coats and hats in sweltering tropical weather, and you have a reasonable idea of most local dogs' physical and mental states.

Their neuroticism takes many forms. For example, one particular dog, a black mongrel bitch, loveable and friendly, was indubitably the fittest, ablest, swiftest and cleverest cat I've ever seen. She was so fast she could catch sparrows on the wing. Often there would be a flock of sparrows hovering and arguing over food scraps on a lawn. There'd be a sudden black streak to scatter the birds and they'd soar away in fright. Either another sparrow died, snapped between the bitch's jaws, or a wounded bird would require nursing for anything from severe shock to a broken wing.

And the very same bitch had the appalling habit of climbing the lower branches of a rose apple tree to torment a resident tree snake. She'd gather the yard-long snake in her mouth, bring it down to ground level and play with it as might a conventional cat with a conventional mouse. She'd release the snake whereupon it would try to escape by slithering away through the grass before having its head suddenly pinned to the ground by a heavy paw. The snake would repeatedly coil and uncoil itself around the bitch's legs. She'd release it again, circle it, feinting as though to attack,

retreat, run at the snake, nose to the ground, wheel away, and suddenly charge it, barking. The snake, visibly angry, head turning in every direction to defend itself, had the same expression, a fleeting mixture of astonishment, frustration and perplexity, I remember adorning the face of a Welsh farmer when he discovered his prize pregnant sow asleep, snoring, drunk out of its mind, on his tractor-shed roof.

The bitch had such a varied repertoire the snake couldn't possibly anticipate her next move. Perhaps she would stand on her hind legs, wag her tail and encircle the snake who'd rapidly be contorting itself into knots. Or she might sit on her haunches, growl and suddenly spring high over the snake's head.

The snake's torment might last anywhere from ten minutes to an hour depending on how quickly the bitch became bored. Eventually she'd ignore the snake and leave in search of new playmates. The snake would return from whence it came. This I could never understand. Of all the trees in which to live the stupid creature favoured the rose apple so that whenever the bitch was in a sadistic mood she knew exactly where to find the snake.

I described her habit of tormenting the snake as appalling, not because it was dangerous to her but because it could be extremely upsetting whenever she decided to invite someone else to play. Too often would she approach strangers with the snake in her mouth and mistaking their frenzied alarm for the start of a new game, pursue them pell-mell through the trees, weaving through the undergrowth, and once she added insult to injury by slobbering all over and licking the face of someone she'd inadvertently tripped during the excitement of chasing them.

She was an accomplished rat-catcher, too, shaming local cats by determinedly pursuing rats wherever they might try to escape. One evening, in death-defying style, she leapt from a balcony into a coconut palm in hot pursuit of an enoromous patriarch with yellow fangs. The tree shuddered and shook, palm fronds crackled and bent, coconuts fell, barks and yelps came from deep within the foliage and then, half falling, half running down the leaning trunk of the tree came herself with one twitching, recently expired rat crushed between her jaws.

She didn't belong to us but then, as far as we could determine, she didn't belong to anyone else either. We'd see her for days on end, contribute to her neuroses by feeding her with leftovers, and then she'd suddenly disappear. Reappearing weeks later, she'd resume the relationship as though she'd never been away, and stay for as long as it suited her. Our relationship was thoroughly relaxed and thankfully never deteriorated to that absurd stage where she took us out for walks.

We had no inkling that the last time we saw her would indeed be the last. Ultimately, conspicuous by her absence, opinions on her fate varied. Found a permanent home, opined a neighbour. No, she must have been stolen, opined another.

I opine nowt. I just hope she's being catty, happily, somewhere.

No book about household animals and insects would be complete without mention, no matter how cursory, of that vermin of vermin, the despicable cockroach. Cockroaches. Ugh. Consider this mention cursory.

Anong tells me that Hilary spent part of the afternoon mumbling, cooing and 'talking' with a frog. I hope he had better luck than me. I've *never* had a rewarding conversation with a frog.

Of all the creatures around the house, frogs are easily the most miserable. They remind me of lonely, embittered old men – the same gloomy preoccupation with themselves.

Something is wrong with the name. Frog is too exotic an appellation, especially for a frog. It conditions one to expect exotic behaviour. Frogs should be called toads and have done with it.

The only time they ever seem mildly enthusiastic is when they croak mantras after heavy thunderstorms. Minutes after a thunderstorm breaks, they emerge from behind rain-filled water jars, leave bathrooms, ponds, stones and other hiding places and journey to the 'district chapel' where they croak monotonously for hours. Heads high, throats puffed, rain-swept mechanical obeisance to their deity.

Only once in their lifetimes, on one occasion only, do they utter a different sound – a high-pitched scream when they are eaten by snakes. If the snake is clumsy, a slow, lingering death follows. It is a gruesome and not uncommon sight.

Wisecracks about frogs and the French apart, there was once something that gave me a frog in my throat for three days thereafter. The something was the most memorable breakfast I have ever *seen.*

It happened during my first year in Thailand. I had spent the night in a whorehouse near Bangkok's docks and was returning home at dawn to grab a few hours' sleep before teaching English to a class of Thai bankers. Before taking a ferry across the river I stopped to drink coffee in a cheap Chinese restaurant where sometimes I ate lunch.

The waterfront restaurant was a typical workingman's eating place with a plain concrete floor upon which were scattered, in no discernible pattern, circular mock-marble-topped tables, wooden stools and tin spittoons. Charcoal stoves stood at the entrance next to tall glass cases imprisoning noodles, meatballs, vegetables, spices, pigs' intestines in various shades of yellow, green and white, and untidy piles of cracked crockery. The walls, upper sections painted a dull institutional green, lower parts made of gleaming lavatory tiles, were covered with faded posters and calendars. Everything was functional and reasonably dirty. Already, in the half-light before the sun rose, the restaurant was crowded with men blearily stirring hot drinks and mechanically chewing soggy pastries. The chill coming off the river made everyone withdraw into themselves. No conversation, just an occasional hacking cough, someone hawking into a spittoon, the noise of river traffic and waves splashing rotten fruit and dead dogs against the bank. The majority of customers were puny-looking Chinese stevedores who unloaded heavy rice sacks from river barges. Everyone looked as though they had spent the night on the tiles.

As I sat waiting for my muddy coffee to cool, and wishing I could somehow avoid the morning's class, a particularly emaciated old stevedore came and sat at my table. Firmly, he placed both hands on the marble table top. His entire body was trembling and his lips were mouthing silent words. Long hairs growing from a wart on his chin were shaking like tassels in a gale.

The restaurant owner, familiar I suppose with all of his regular customers' wants, opened his cavernous refrigerator and extracted a bottle of 7-Up. He opened it and came over to our table, placing the heavily iced bottle, a spoon, a glass and two muck-stained duck eggs on a plate before the trembling old man.

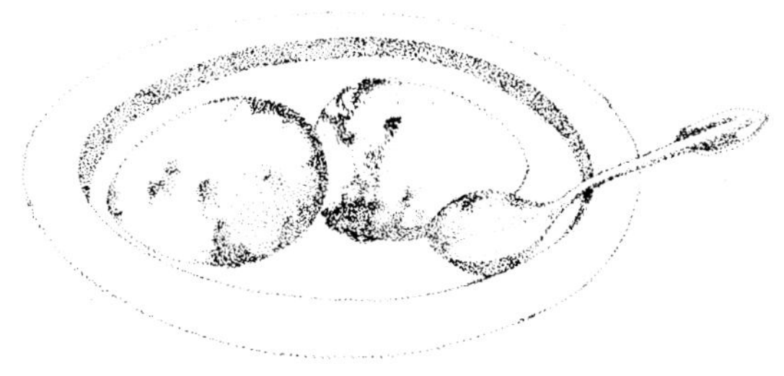

The old man stared at the plate for some time. His eyes were rheumy, pink. His eyebrows were virtually bald. His few remaining teeth were as prominent as those on a skeleton, black or gold molars and grey, transparent gums. His neck was flaccid, mottled, like a plucked turkey's. His hairy ears were lobeless and he was wearing a soiled undershirt like those used in detergent commercials. A sight. The 'morning-after' personified. Still engaged in some profound inner dialogue.

The cogs in his mind must have shuddered, meshed and brought the restaurant back into focus because, then, deliberately, he broke the raw eggs into the glass. They sank and settled like baleful orange eyes; to the eggs he added the sparkling 7-Up; and then two heaped spoonsful of hotter-than-hell red and green chillies. Holding the glass in one hand he stirred the concoction with the other, the sound of spoon against glass in his trembling hands like a scrambled and very urgent morse code message. The mixture increasingly resembled an internal haemorrhage.

I couldn't believe the man was serious. I was an impressionable twenty-two. The Orient was a new and exciting place to me. But this? Jesus Christ. Was I witnessing the ablution of some esoteric Eastern sect? Was the man a Chinese Hindu? An ascetic? A masochist? Mad? In one swift movement he opened his throat, swallowed the mixture in one gulp and expectantly held out his hand. The restaurant owner promptly reappeared with a half-pint glass one-third full with neat Thai rice whisky. The old man virtually snatched the glass away and poured the whisky down his throat. It was like watching someone swallow a fatal dose of poison and then immediately swallow the antidote. His eyes watered, his eyeballs momentarily disappearing like submerged pieces of wood and then floating back to the surface again. He sniffed. And then gave the restaurant owner the exact amount of money, about nine ounces of small coins. A barely suppressed belch; nose delicately, no words can describe *how* delicately, pinched between forefinger and thumb, the despatch of first phlegm and then snot in the general direction of a spittoon. Standing up, now audibly muttering, he exited.

I asked the restaurant owner if the old man 'ate' like that very often.

'Two or three times a day.'

'Everyday?'

'Everyday.'

'Doesn't he ever eat anything else?'

'Sometimes he treats himself to plate of peppered rice soaked with soybean milk and raw garlic.'

'Nothing else?'

'No. Not here at least.'

'How long's he been eating like this?'

'Oh, about seven years.'

Over the years I continued to eat at the restaurant. One day I asked the owner if the same character still came in.

'No. He's at sea.'

That I could believe. 'Doing what?'

'His friends told me he got a job on a coastal steamer as a cook.'

Maybe our thoughts were similar. We both laughed. Somewhere, if they survived the first week, the crew of one particular coastal steamer is dining, I am sure, on the most inventive cuisine *anywhere.* They must be an admirable bunch.

Birds. Taken for granted, yet without them the orchards would seem like graveyards. Very few known by name. Songsters are more often heard than seen, afternoon duets, tree top solos, kitchen roof recitals, or chatter, chatter beneath the eaves. Hundreds of sparrows.

Sparrows preen themselves on the balcony rail, beaks foraging under wings. They wing away, frequently returning to take short rests. Others huddle against each other on electric cables and telephone wires, unemployed actors awaiting auditions. When rain streams down they shelter under the balcony roof, shoulders hunched, looking every bit as disconsolate as a soaked, silent bus queue. Skulls move as though they are watching slow motion tennis.

A sparrow's nest beneath the eaves in threatened by a tokay. Squawking parents try to keep the lizard away, flying close to it, but careful to keep out of range of powerful jaws. The tokay regards them disdainfully, as might an elephant pestered by rabbits. If it had wings there would be a massacre. The sparrows are unsuccessful at keeping the tokay at bay and it reaches the nest. Shrill cries and the birds fly away.

In a clearing in the orchards is a pile of stones originally planned to be the foundations of a house. The house has never been built and the stones have never been used, except as a refuge for rats and as a place where birds drop enormous water snails to break their shells. Bleached snail shells,

like fragments of mother-of-pearl, litter the ground. Becoming to its designation as a cemetery, the area is very quiet.

Under the eaves of a neighbourhood monastery chapel, a disturbed owl glares at intruders with withering superiority. Looking like a taxidermist's nightmare, an orange, pink and green bird perches on the uppermost branch of a guava tree, silent, aloof, swaying in a breeze. A hawk lazily circles, I wish, I wish I could do the same, gliding, high above the trees, black against the sky.

A ten-second drama as three screeching, excitable birds, black plumage, bright yellow beaks, espy a beautifully marked green snake moving along the top of a fence. In rapid succession they dive-bomb the snake, claws opened before them. With equal speed the snake strikes at each bird, moving and defending itself simultaneously. The birds are careful, too careful, aiming to catch the snake by the neck. Each time they pass over, the snake twists its neck and angrily strikes backwards. Too exposed, the snake half falls, half slithers down a post into dense undergrowth. The birds circle, denied a meal, settle atop the fence and look down into the undergrowth, frustrated. Always miss . . . too careful. A chattering analysis, exaggerated take-offs, flap away. The snake has completely vanished.

Frequently sparrows fly into the house and are unable to find their way out, flying from one room to another, upstairs and downstairs. They perch and look perplexed, fly to different corners, completely confused. Anong is an expert bird-catcher. Delightedly, she cups the sparrow in her hands, admires it, gently strokes its head. Shows it to Hilary who chuckles, makes a clumsy grab for it. Sparrow passive, silent. Anong walks onto the balcony, opens her hands and the sparrow flies away. Hilary laughs. Anong watches it fly to a tree and turns around wearing a wide, happy grin. Contagious. I feel happy, too.

Shaving. Out of the corner of the eye, a strange sight. Oh, no. Armageddon. A snake with legs. But it is only a bathroom coloniser, a millipede. Scrape. Scrape. Curse this rusted super stainless steel razor blade. Grimly determined, the millipede moves out of vision.

An unusual story in a local newspaper recently. A train on what was once known as 'Death Railway' (the line built by the Japanese with prisoner-of-war labour to connect Siam and Burma) was delayed for half an hour by millipedes. Some distance from a station the train driver noticed the rails were red and stopped the train. Increduously, he saw 'thousands of millipedes on the rails and sleepers'. He set the train in motion once more but after a few yards the wheels lost traction as mashed millipedes oiled the track. The driver reversed the train and requested the passengers to leave. Then, several times, he charged the train into the swarming millipedes and finally broke through. The story omitted further mention of the passengers. Presumably, to rejoin the train, they were obliged to wade ankle deep through masses of massacred millipedes. Ergh.

What a strange world this is. A cockroach goes to the moon. Millipedes delay a train. And super stainless steel razor blades rust within three days.

With disarming simplicity a Thai geography textbook states: '. . .wherever in Thailand water is found, fish are found.' It's amazingly true. And it's never been proved it doesn't rain fish. Here. During the rainy season, when water collects and forms pools around the house, the fish population must treble. A few days after heavy rain a six-inch deep virgin pool is aswarm with various water-insects, is host to journeying crabs and frogs, and contains fish – half-inch, half-gold, half-transparents that have suddenly materialised from nowhere. The water is replenished daily by rainfall, the fish prosper and grow large enough to attract cats' and children's attention. Even if the pool is independent, unconnected to pools known to contain fish, is not much larger than a puddle, fish miraculously appear. From where? '. . .wherever in Thailand water is found, fish are found.' There is probably a perfectly irrational explanation.

One year *John 2* and the kitchen were flooded. Anong and I saw a couple of snakes swim past the back door and at one point the water in the kitchen was nearly a foot deep. After a week, when the waters had receded, we discovered the squat-type toilet bowl brimful with tiny fish busily gobbling mosquito larvae.

Permanent pools scattered throughout the orchards contain fish that many tropical-fish enthusiasts would gladly add to their aquariums. Close to banks where palm tree roots plunge like nerve endings into sun-dappled waters, fish make pouting ascents to the surface and slowly sink, gill fins feathered like aircraft propellors. Surface microdots of flame green separate from a ripple made by a turtle or large fish and a dragonfly zigzags above the waters. Red ants march up and down half-submerged palm fronds. In intricate shadows and shade the water is black, in sunlight a pale bottle-green. Overhead, birds sing and leaves shiver in the wind. The sky is a blue and green canopy. Screened from the outside world, the ponds are self-contained worlds of incessant activity.

Anong bought two goldfish for Hilary when he was six months old. Conscientiously, we fed them daily with mosquito larvae collected from nearby pools. Within a week we were itching and scratching, slapping and cursing. Uneaten larvae swiftly matured until the house resembled a mosquito farm. We have never yet decided which was worse – a new bite every minute or the smell of much, much incense, supposedly a mosquito deterrent, that perfumed the house so much it seemed like the temple of some highly decadent religion.

If ever I am in the company of anglers who tell 'fishy' stories, I shall tell them the following tale. Late one rainy-season evening, returning from the main road to the house, I saw a fish *walking* across the track. The fish, a dark catfish, moved into undergrowth bordering the track. My mind, sober as it was, refused to believe what my eyes had seen. I was in two minds – actually, I was in many – whether to tell Anong what I had seen. I decided to shape my observation in the form of a question.

I arrived home.

'Anong, what is the name of the fish that walks?'

'Have you been drinking?'

'Don't be silly. What is it called?'

'What is what called?'

'The fish that walks.'

'You *have* been drinking.'

'Look, I saw a fish walking across. . .'

'Your breath doesn't smell. Vodka?'

'. . .the track. It was brown and had. . .'

'There's no need to lie. How many did you have?'

'. . .a beard. Well, whiskers.'

The last sentence sent her into hysterics. By the time she had stopped laughing I was furious.

'A fish with a beard?'

'Whiskers.'

'Make up your mind!'

'Whiskers. Whiskers. Long-twirling-freaking whiskers!'

'Take an asprin and go to bed. You'll feel much better tomorrow.'

'Whiskers. A catfish walking! What's the name of it!!?'

'Temper, temper. Calm down.'

'Who's angry?'

'You. And drunk.'

I gave up.

That weekend we were shopping at the local market. Walking between stalls, the sight of a brown heap. Strewn across a trestle were hundreds of them. Walking catfish.

'That's it! That's it!!'

'That's what?'

'The fish that walks!'

'That doesn't walk.'

'It does. I saw one four nights ago.'

'It doesn't walk.'

'It does.'

'It doesn't.'

'It *does.*'

'It *doesn't.* It crawls.'

'Jesus Christ.'

'It crawls. It needs legs to walk. Anyone can see it doesn't have legs. It crawls.'

'Jesus Christ.'

A few months later we were aboard a boat going to a small island. I forget the subject of conversation but simultaneously we both saw a flying fish break surface, skim across the sea and belly-flop from view. We looked at each other without speaking and turned to look at the sea again. Another flying fish broke surface. Private memories. We both sat in a tight-lipped, bloody-minded silence. And then laughed. And laughed. And laughed. People thought we'd had a few.

Each time I sort old canvases stored in the dark corners of an outhouse, I disturb tiny, almost transparent scorpions. Anong tells me they're sold by the kilogramme in a local market. Makes sense, I suppose. If you can't beat 'em, eat 'em. I'll never forget a euphoric barefoot walk through Angkor Wat by moonlight when I nearly trod on one the size of a lobster, metallic silver, claws wide apart ready to strike. End of euphoria.

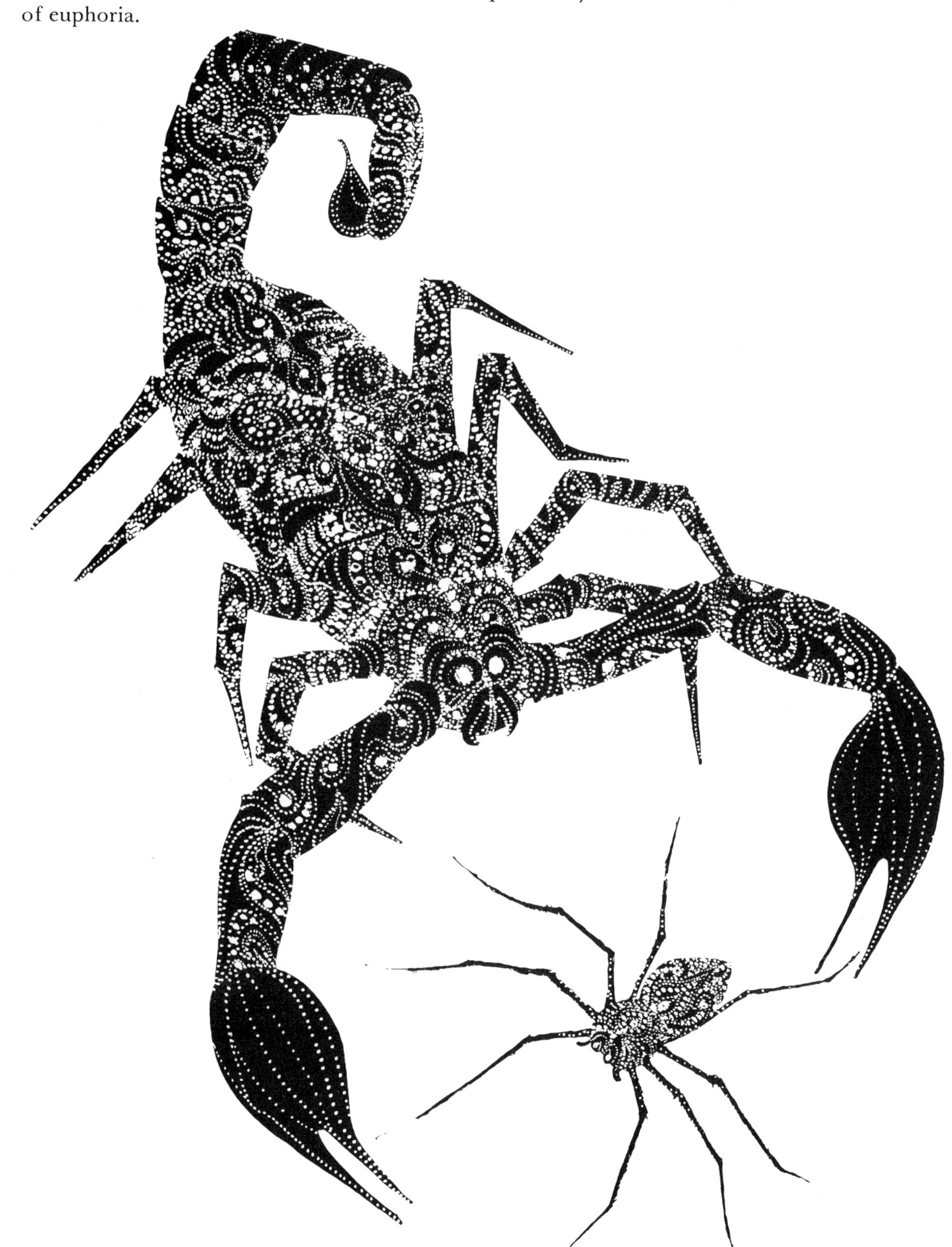

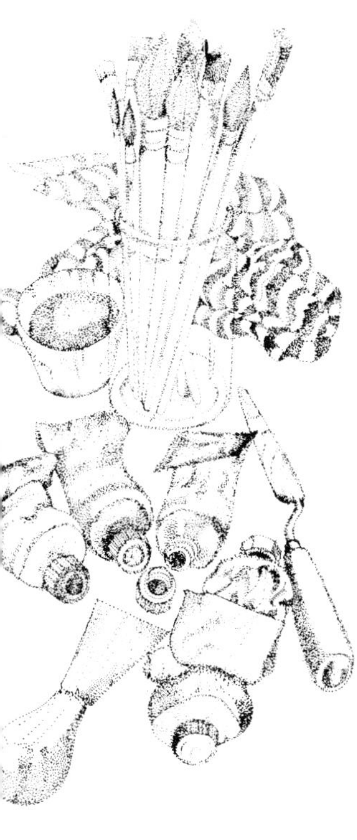

I was supposed to have finished a painting for someone today. But I didn't. I spent the morning reading the latest T. McGee adventure instead. Entertaining and excellent value for money, as always.

In the afternoon, Kasem the snake man dropped by. We sat on the balcony drinking gallons of hot tea and during one part of the afternoon Kasem, ever alert for snakes, spotted one painfully swallowing a lizard half its length and more than three times its girth. The drama unfolded in a tree touching the balcony.

We spent a pleasant afternoon chatting about various things – nothing of any great importance.

A 39-year-old Thai Moslem, Kasem is one of my favourite people, someone whose company I invariably enjoy. I had first met him through a mutual friend, another Thai Moslem. Although a Moslem I am not, I know many of them because I enjoy Moslem food so much. And, *non sequitur* that it is, I generally fast during *Ramadan,* the annual fast that lasts for thirty days, when Moslems deny themselves food, liquids and cigarettes during daylight hours and attempt to lead exemplary lives in the hope that by so doing they will find themselves closer to God.

What generally happens to me as a result of trying to be completely honest with myself and others, controlling my anger in all situations, endeavouring to remain mentally pure, refraining from pleasurable activities – watching films, listening to music, reading, drinking booze, over-eating, not to mention a self-imposed celibacy – for thirty consecutive days is that I become extremely tired, hungry, thirsty, irascible, bored, sexually frustrated, increasingly neurotic and conclude the fast with the conviction that all it achieves is to screw up my mind even more.

Being totally honest is downright dangerous. Most of the people I know, myself included, are so accustomed to lying through their teeth ninety per cent of the time that breaking the habit and telling the truth is as painful and physically hazardous as undergoing cold turkey. I mean, when I have to tell the truth to total strangers I really fear for my personal safety. I can remember countless ocasions when I have mindlessly and recklessly told the truth and consequently suffered ostracism, mental anguish, remorse, guilt and *real* pain. On one occasion I awoke in a hospital bed in India with miles of transparent plastic tubing, leading from bottles and flasks and tanks, inserted into my nostrils and into or out of my anus (I have never been able to decide if they were connected or not, the tubes I mean, not my nostrils and anus (yours are, too)) because I had truthfully told the anaesthetist that I have had a long history of respiratory problems (lung abcess, asthma, bronchitis, etc.) and please to be very careful when anaesthetising me for the appendicitis operation I was about to undergo and naturally he had not believed a single word I said because I entered the operating theatre on a Monday afternoon and woke up in an intensive-care-unit bed the following Saturday.

One thing I like about Kasem is that he lives on the fringe of society rather than in the middle of it. For example, the only book he reads is the Koran – no other literature, no books, no magazines, no newspapers and no advertisements. Moreover, he does not listen to news broadcasts on the radio because a radio he does not possess. He is supremely ignorant about politics; current events; economic developments (though he appreciates things are getting more expensive), scientific discoveries; fashion; life styles; women's lib; water beds; unisex; The Flat Earth Society; transcendental meditation; IATA inflight regulations; streaking or comparative religion, etcetera, etcetera, an ignorance that indubitably contributes to his self-contained contentment. Ignorance is *not* bliss but it certainly helps.

Accordingly, he is not burdened with second or third-hand arguments about politics, inflation, foreign policy, ecological balance, the communist threat or price warfare and, spared the constant bombardment of hard fact and misinformation spewed forth by the local and international communications media, is free of the normal, maladjusted, everyday anxieties suffered by an increasingly large segment of the world's population generally classified as the 'educated and well-informed'.

Kasem does not wake up sweating in the middle of the night to worry about the future, deferred payments, mortages, tax fiddles,

investments, expense accounts, projected sales targets, promotions, bonuses, sabbaticals, recalcitrant children, real estate values, college fees, impotence, allowances, a second car, golf handicaps, medical check-ups, bridge partners, excessive cholesterol, duodenal ulcers, breast cancer or retirement schemes.

Neither does he feel any guilt, remorse, anxiety or regret about Hitler's treatment of the Jews, the plight of U.S. Negroes, the wartime internment of American Japanese, the rape of Tibet, Hungary or Czechoslovakia, the atomic bombs dropped on Japan, the massacres of Red Indians, the Palestinian problem or the starving millions in Asia.

In writing this I am reminded of someone at the opposite end of the spectrum, a Scottish acquaintance who is the creative director at one of Bangkok's largest advertising agencies. Considering his advantages – an excellent education, an extremely well-paid, secure position, his own house, a very attractive family and all the material comforts anyone could ever wish for – he is extraordinarily maladjusted to the twentieth century and would have been immeasurably more comfortable living in Ashoke's India or Cleopatra's Egypt either as an itinerant peanut seller or as an embalmer attached to one of the royal pyramids.

He has, I have gathered over the years, innumerable obsessions. He wonders if he is enough of a hero to his children, is totally hypochondriac, suffers continually from constipation, worries excessively about his driving habits, diet, shoe leather, others' opinions of him, his sexual capacity and performance, creative talents and God knows what else, and sinks into recurring bouts of depression whenever he reads in the newspapers of assaults, blackmail, murder, strikes, invasions, terrorism, demonstrations, assassinations and political chicanery. He worries constantly about raising children in such an imperfect world, broods and speculates endlessly about their futures – whether they will be able to find good jobs and trustworthy spouses – believes himself to be a poor father and is utterly convinced he will be an even worse grandparent. . .it goes on and on and on. To catalogue his worries, complaints and neuroses would take the combined efforts of the chief librarian and research staff of the British Museum well into the next century.

Obviously, he is far and away too literate for his own good. The charming, talented, intelligent and poor misguided fool literally believes every word he reads.

Not yet thirty years old, he is in many ways prematurely senile. He seriously doubts if he will be able to programme his life profitably during his retirement (!) and lives in pure terror of the prospect of countless hours of old-age boredom. In an effort to do something about it he dissipates his present energy by hopping from one hobby to another – wine-making, Chinese calligraphy, model-building, learning Spanish, Greek and Urdu, cooking Ethiopian and Bolivian delicacies, collecting whistles, kidney stones, cigar labels and African tribal dildoes, compiling discographies of all jazzmen with names beginning with Y, studying apricot farming, writing twenty-three unfinished novels and trying his hand at poetry, producing convoluted, maudlin verse that for a time, dressed in a kilt and sporran, exposing himself to the risk of physical violence, he recited aloud in various Bangkok bars accompanied by terse multilingual threats — in the hope of discovering something that will keep him fully occupied and, by association, *alive,* thirty years hence.

Utterly brainwashed by contemporary literature, he can't meet Negroes without feeling sexually inadequate and insecure and a bit afraid and consequently, in a reversal of historical roles, turns into a babbling sycophantic Uncle Tom whenever he is in their company. Once I heard him spouting wild-eyed praise of natural rhythms and sensuality and the ineffable superiority of black athletes and the alluring, timeless mystique of the dark continent to two bemused and mildly frightened Fijiian seamen.

He feels intensely guilty whenever he meets Indians and Pakistanis and forthrightly apologises for 347 years of British misrule and economic exploitation and is effusive in his praise of the *Kama Sutra,* mutton curries, Gandhi and a treasured scale miniature of the Taj Mahal that was made in Bombay from human toenails.

Because he must somehow clear his head of all the faeces therein he suffers from compulsive verbal diarrohea. You get the picture.

He mixes tranquilizers and alcohol with such abandon that his metabolism must veer between that of a 200-year-old turtle and a panic-stricken monkey. Being in his company makes me nervous. Every situation, event and argument he participates in must be competitive and challenging in nature. He expects and even demands when I am with him a dynamic and aggressive response on my part. I will not oblige. Besides, the mental energy I expend in religiously lying to him exhausts me.

I find it impossible, distasteful even, to tell him the truth about any damn thing. I would certainly not want the responsibility of being the one to answer his fearful and neurotic questions honestly, thereby causing him to flip his lid, freak out, twist his mental knickers or send him around that proverbial bend. I honestly believe that my lying reassurances are of greater value in helping consolidate whatever shred of sanity he may still miraculously possess than any truths, no matter how subtle or oblique. The truth might destroy him: it would certainly be cruel and I do not subscribe to that nonsense about it sometimes being necessary to be cruel to be kind. The concept that cruelty can sometimes be equated with kindness is another of those enduring stupidities to which people cling — like 'crime never pays' or 'honesty is the best policy'.

Being in Kasem's company is totally different — relaxing, refreshing, entertaining and pleasant. He is really one of the few people I can tell the truth to with confidence. I can be completely honest about anything and everything without fearing obscene repercussions or vulgar visitations of remorse or guilt. And, not burdened with a competitive need to prove the possession of a superman's intellect, or extreme sensitivity, or a pain-in-the-ass social conscience, Kasem is abnormally natural.

Enough self-indulgence for one day. . . .

I suspect that after the birth of their first child many new parents enjoy different visual perceptions. Personally, anything newborn attracted my attention more readily after the birth of my son. Hitherto common occurences such as young chinchoks dropping from ceilings or the sight of baby frogs became visually more precious; and emotions nurtured by Hilary's birth embraced things that previously had seemed impersonal. New shoots on a plant, a pregnant woman (please be careful with your precious cargo), mosquito larvae wriggling in half a coconut shell of water, an eggladen spider, an unseen child disconsolately sobbing – all, and many more, touched a newborn nerve precipitating a happiness sometimes tinged with a subtle melancholy.

A case in point during post-birth contentment was the arrival at the house of a pregnant cat. It simply appeared one day and adopted us. After exploring the house it slept under the stairs, an open space in one of the kitchen walls, making a plastic washing bowl its bed. Less than a week later it gave birth to four kittens.

I became fond of it and the litter, unusual because previously I had neither liked nor disliked cats. They simply left me cold. An old friend, a hirsute Canadian anthropologist, had once tried to convert me without success. During a beery evening in an open-air restaurant – both of us were pickled – a cat walked past, looked at me and jumped onto my lap. A mere reflex action, I brushed it off and shooed it away. My friend appeared personally offended and asked me if I prefered dogs to cats. I nodded. He promptly informed me that I and people like me harbour a stupid preference and launched into a long pro-cat, anti-dog tirade. 'Cats are independent, emotionally stable, intelligent and clean. Dogs are stupid, dependent on man, dirty and neurotic.' He passionately denounced dog-loving societies and mouthed lots of abstruse blah about noble savages. Finally he exhausted himself and ordered more beer. Presently he is in Nova Scotia surrounded, I imagine, by cats and quaffing beer laced with sherry.

One day the kittens left their washing bowl and, escorted by their attentive mother, explored the ground floor of the house. At times it seemed there were a dozen of them. They trapped themselves behind the refrigerator, slid across the tiled floor of the main bathroom, played with live electric wires, sat in a charcoal bucket, wrestled with each other, ate their mother's food, chewed grass and puked everywhere, and inspected each new object with wide-eyed wonder.

Often during their excursions they got underfoot but toleration was well above normal levels and nothing mattered. They did what kittens will and matured with astonishing speed, astonishing when you compare them with humans. Eventually their mother left and the tribe disintegrated. A noodle seller took one, a neighbour one, one we gave to a Buddhist monk in a nearby monastery and the remaining kitten-cum-adult, who showed affection for her birthplace, drowned herself in a water jar. We buried her behind the house. The grave is still there, yet another of the house's physical reminders of emotional attachments — a flecked ceiling made when a can of paint exploded like a champagne bottle, scratches on the floor when Hilary's cot was delivered, etc.

Recently, I received a letter from my friend. Now he is living in Australia, encumbered with a Ph.D. (his phrase, not mine), teaching, and researching a paper for some esoteric organisation on 'The Artistic Consequences Of The Drinking Habits Of The Indigenous & Immigrant Aborigines'. He mentions that in his spare time he breeds Alsatians. Certain he was frustrated at being unable to find a cat that barked. Turncoat.

I have seen only three living centipedes here. Twice I saw them outdoors, each time on wet, windswept afternoons when they appeared every bit as nasty as their reputations. The third time was inside the house, sitting on top of a stool watching Anong wield a hammer with erratic accuracy as she leapt about pounding a writhing centipede, about nine inches long, into pulp in front of the refrigerator door. The thing had had the temerity and misfortune to emerge from underneath the refrigerator as Anong was rummaging in the deep freeze compartment. Never have I seen my wife move so fast; nor kill anything with such obvious relish. A reduced centipede population is for the common good: bang, Bang, BANG. The centipede jerked like a piece of wrinkled, wet elastic each time the hammer fell. Finally a wrangled mess remained and Anong wept softly, emotionally exhausted.

I know a Buddhist monk who accidentally trod on a centipede and who stoically suffered the painful consequences. I have been told that centipedes eat cockroaches. If true, that is at least one BIG thing in their favour.

Muang revisited us. On her third Hilary-cradling, crab-hunting day she asked us if we could take her to Nakorn Pathom, a medium-sized town about thirty-five miles west of Bangkok. Nakorn Pathom's main attraction is an enormous pagoda which is the world's tallest Buddhist monument. Muang had never been there, wished to, and we agreed. We made the mid-week journey the following day.

The pagoda is set within terraced grounds and during the week is a pleasant place to visit. The courtyards and galleries, full of architectural and sculptural interest, are quiet. Large, shade-giving trees dot the area and the orange-tiled pagoda towers above the complex to dominate the surrounding countryside. The innermost courtyard is especially pleasing. Except for birdsong and the soft tinkling of small, breeze-swept bronze bells it is peacefully silent and nothing can be seen or heard of the outside world other than treetops and open sky.

At many of Thailand's popular religious shrines you can have your fortune told. Nakorn Pathom is no exception. Daily, scattered about the pagoda, sitting in the shade of large trees or leaning against cool walls, their paraphernalia piled on reed mats, palmists quietly confer with clients, many of whom are middle-aged spinsters.

A common species in Thailand, many palmists lead highly profitable existences since innumerable Thais and Chinese consult them regularly, seeking directions on a multitude of problems. In much the same way that people have family doctors, many families have family palmists. The consequences of their predictions are sometimes surprising.

I'm always reminded of a Thai acquaintance whose wife's attitude to him suddenly changed. She had long tolerated his nightly drinking bouts with old cronies but suddenly began interrogating him closely every night when he returned home. She demanded to know what he had been doing, with whom, where he had been. Soon bored with her constant bickering

the husband delivered an ultimatum, in effect ordering her to shut up or tell him what was bothering her. Eventually she confessed that her regular palmist had predicted that her husband was *certain* to take a mistress during the current year. Angered, the husband's first impulse was to go and throttle the palmist for interfering with his home life. But soon he calmed down and regarded the prediction with contemptuous amusement. Within a matter of months, however, constantly brooding on the prediction, whether to fulfill it or not, or to spite his wife (not even he is sure), he finally did it. He took a mistress. Naturally enough, his wife, on discovering this, was sorely disappointed. *But:* her faith in the palmist was immeasurably strengthened. Every cloud has a silver lining. . .

I have little faith in palmistry even though during the time I lived in India a wizened old man in a yoga ashram made several accurate predictions concerning my future in Thailand. (He was just the exception who proved the rule.) However, Anong, like many Thai friends, is, despite repeated denials to the contrary, a firm believer.

Anyway, during this visit to Nakorn Pathom, impulsively, I approached one of the plamists, choosing an old, old man who seemed, purely by appearance, to be the most knowledgeable, and asked him to predict my future. I sat cross-legged in front of him and waited as he cleaned his wire-framed spectacles, fastidiously arranged them on the tip of his nose and spread a schoolchild's lined exercise book on the mat between us. Date and time of birth established, he leafed through a dog-eared book and consulted several charts. Periodically, he traced the main lines of my hands with a pencil as he sought information on which to base his calculations. He jotted several notes in his exercise book and after about five minutes began to tell me the usual pleasantries about greater wealth, good health and a long, happy life.

Meanwhile, Anong had taken Hilary into the pagoda's main chapel, left him there with Muang and had come over to where I was sitting. She had been standing quietly behind me for a couple of minutes. Suddenly she asked the palmist if I was married.

He looked up, thinking, I suppose, that she was just a curious bystander and answered, 'No, not yet.'

Anong's eyes narrowed. 'Interesting. When will he marry?'

Another look at my hands. 'Not for a long time. Not until he is at least thirty-five.'

'And?'

'Then he will have two wives. But no children.'

'How do you figure that out?'

Pointing to my hands, 'It says so here.'

'He's definitely not married, huh?'

'No, definitely not.'

'Are you sure?'

'Of course,' irritably, 'I am sure.'

'And who do you suppose I am?'

An expletive. Impatiently, 'How the hell should I know?'

'*I* am his wife.'

Startled, the palmist shook his head. 'No.'

'I *am.*'

The palmist peered intently at my face, trying hard to discern any kind of expression that might betray a relationship with this strange woman. With some difficulty, I managed to keep a straight face. And then raised my eyebrows enquiringly. The palmist looked immensely relieved. He shook his head again. 'No' triumphantly. He glared at Anong, stole another glance at my hands and repeated, 'No,' emphatically.

'I am his. . .'

'No.'

'Why,' icily, 'should I claim to be his wife if I am not?'

'Listen, lady, I've heard people claim they're the Buddha reborn. . .'

An angry snort. Anong walked away in disgust. I thanked the man, pressed twenty baht (one US dollar) into his hand and hurried after her. I caught up with her on the long flight of steps to the main chapel. She was swearing softly under her breath.

'How much did you pay that idiot?'

'Twenty baht.'

'What a waste of money! The man is five hundred kinds of a fol!'

'Granted. But if all his predictions are so inaccurate he can't have too many customers. I expect he needs all the money he can get. Besides, it's worth paying twenty baht just to be told that one is still a carefree bachelor with a great future.'

'Harrruuuuuumph.'

'Look, why don't *you* go to another fortune teller and see what he says?'

'Certainly not.'

'Chicken.'

'I am *not.*'

'Yes you are. If he tells you you're not married yet and you'll have two husbands but no children you'll . . .'

'O.K. I'm chicken.'

Later, that evening, relaxing at home, thumbing through the local newspaper. Reach the woman's page, skim through the 'Dear Gabby' agony column, ignore the social news and spot the day's horoscope. I don't really believe in horoscopes *either* but generally check because there *might* be good news coming my way. Gemini. The day's entry concludes '. . .and a third party will confuse issues between you and your marriage partner.'

Hot damn.

'Winter. . . the loveliest time of the year. Snow softly falls to blanket everything. A mantle of white softens edges and crowns the spiky heads of palm trees. Coconuts look like marzipanned bonbons. Banana trees shrug off the sparkling powder until it collects in deep drifts at their feet. Mango trees sag, dark leaves peeking from cascades of snow, melted and refrozen to look like icing sugar.

'Coconuts drop noiselessly into drifts, leaving holes swiftly filled by tumbling snow. Lotuses stand in dark, thin-iced waters, pink and orange heads vibrant colours under pale winter sunshine. Hawkers' cries are amplified by the still air. All sounds become razor-sharp.

'Some animals experience difficulty in moving around. Tokays and chinchoks tread warily and remain inside houses most of the time, only young and daring lizards venturing outside where they slide down icicles and fall deep into the snow. In fact, around the outskirts of houses, imprints of surprised lizard shapes, spreadeagled as they fell, are common. Chattering with pleasure, lizards return inside houses and repeat their performances so that quiet mornings are punctuated by soft plops of fallen bodies and squeals of delight.

'The orchards are very quiet. There is little movement. The few distant sounds are all man-made.

'At night no moths hover outside lighted windows. No frogs croak. No mosquitos bite. No dogs howl. No chinchoks hunt. Silence, a deafening silence outside. The world is a deserted museum.

'Keeping warm taxes ingenuity. The poor light fires. There are few *old* wooden houses in Thailand: annually they are burnt down to warm people. In many neighbourhoods houseowners pool houses for fuel. Whole streets disappear within a week as houses are systematically set ablaze to provide warmth for a shivering population. Entire districts go up in flames as numb itinerants travel from one bonfire to another. For six weeks of the year fire-brigades daren't show their faces. Old-timers tell of an occasion before World War Two when an eager, inexperienced crew began to extinguish one blaze and was very nearly lynched for its efforts.

'Heat melts the snow which refreezes and transforms many erstwhile towns and villages into treacherous sheets of ice. People walk very carefully. During winter one shouts greetings to acquaintances at a distance of twenty yards because without warning they often slip and slide past or away at great speed.

'During this time the crime rate drops to zero because people are too preoccupied with keeping warm. And traffic accidents are non-existent because there is no traffic. No one drives since the experience of one adventurous spirit at the turn of the century. Many, many years ago, when the motor car was first introduced to Siam, a Chinese merchant attempted to drive through snowbound Bangkok. Everything went well until the first time he was obliged to brake. Then he went into a long, graceful, sideways skid, bounced off buildings, felled all the trees in one avenue, travelled in several directions and, battered and bruised, finally came to rest against an icebound merchant vessel on the frozen river.

'The sound of metal against metal thundered upstream and downstream and awoke murderous headaches among crew members sleeping off hangovers in their cabins. Reverberations of the collision were felt all over the city. A court composer, temporarily deserted by inspiration, noted the melody produced by his tinkling chandelier and penned one of the most popular tunes of the period. In a city kitchen a chef was astonished to see his cage of songbirds plunge from the ceiling into a tureen of boiling water. Sampling the concoction afterwards, he smacked his lips and realised the dish was a culinary triumph.

'The unfortunate driver abandoned his vehicle and, accompanied by the curses of haggard seamen, staggered ashore. Wandering some way inland, he fell to his knees in a field cleared of snow for a royal parade. There prostrated, thanking his lucky stars for his escape, absent-mindedly chewing and kissing blades of grass, he failed to notice the arrival of a conscientious policeman who promptly arrested him and escorted him to the nearest police station. There the driver suffered the ultimate indignity of being the first – and the only – person ever charged with illegally grazing on a royal pasture. His uninsured vehicle was gradually blown downstream by violent winds that nightly whistled across the ice and a month later the vehicle sank at the mouth of the estuary.

'Animal activity is also suspended, so much so that some creatures treble their natural life spans during the season. For people, there are a few hardships like eating frozen curries which can be as unpleasant as eating hot ice cream. Generally, everyone is cheerful.

'After the thaw, life returns to normal. Animals hunt, cars collide, the crime rate soars, birds sing, the sun boils, houses are rebuilt, lovers rendezvous secretly, air-conditioners are turned on full blast – the normal rhythms pulsate.'

Christmas day. If we've heard 'I'm Dreaming Of A White Christmas' on the radio once, we've heard it ten times. The temperature is nearly 90° F. Not a single cloud, let alone a snowflake in sight. Plum pudding and ice-cold local beer a heady combination make. . .

Coconut trees girdled with tin. Nibbled cakes of soap. Shredded, moist paper beneath the stairs. Yellow teeth, brown-black pelts, squeak, squeak. Rats.

Loners. Ship-in-a-bottle, rat through a hole. Elastic girth, slim, slim, slimmer but fierce, oh yes, fierce. Stand off cats. Noses to the ground, fast movements, hop, skip, crunch, squeak. Buck teeth chew refuse, away along fence tops, under houses, into undergrowth, corporeal ghosts in moonlight, black phantoms, scratch and scratch, disgust me as much as cockroaches, don't need poison, a cat or traps, just a tame snake.

Tame snake.

After four days of grey, dry, oppressive weather during which heavy, rain-swollen clouds have concealed the sun, moon and stars, the heavens have finally opened and it has rained incessantly all day. I am returning home at night by taxi. Several roads and lanes are flooded. Countless shopfronts are awash and partly submerged. Some have been emptied, goods hurriedly stored upstairs. In others, unlucky merchants glumly watch merchandise floating and bobbing in the wakes of passing cars. Bars and restaurants are tightly packed with commuters patiently waiting for the storm to exhaust itself. Non-concrete roads are already disintegrating. Axle-deep water conceals potholes into which many unwary drivers lurch. Their stalled vehicles cause horrendous traffic jams. A ten-minute journey takes an hour. Taxi fares have doubled or trebled. Tempers are steadily rising.

The storm increases in violence as rain streaks across our bonnet in windswept flourishes, lashing the windscreen and windows with extraordinary force, and drumming the roof in incessant fury. Thunder continually roars, and lightning, far brighter than any Hollywood special effect, dramatically illuminates the black night. Our lethargic windscreen wipers struggle to cope with the deluge; our headlights isolate a bewildering pattern of indistinct shapes, scurrying pedestrians, coloured reflections from shop windows and neon signs and the blinding dazzle of oncoming vehicles.

The interior of our tightly closed cab is airless, uncomfortable and wet. The roof constantly drips and dribbles and water slops and gurgles around our ankles as it bubbles up through a rust-ridden floor. Our brakes have almost ceased functioning and with monotonous regularity the engine moans, whines, shudders and screams in protest. I sit impatiently, silently grinding my teeth as the taxi inches forward.

I am hoping, against all odds, to arrive home before Hilary, now ten months old, goes to bed. Earlier in the day he stood up for the first time, took one tentative step and fell flat on his face. Fantastic. A four-minute mile next!

Just the sight of him happily grinning will compensate for a totally unproductive day. I've travelled far too many miles to hear far too many excuses – like the Chinese frame maker who couldn't finish some canvases for me because, he said, his chief assistant's father's best friend was hospitalised after an eleventh-century Buddha image fell on his head when he was planting carrots, obliging his chief assistant to travel upcountry to somewhere near Hanoi to exercise his father's best friend's elephant.

As we cross the river my Thai taxi driver is peering intently through the windscreen, using the slow-moving and fluid red tail lights of the taxi in

front as a guide. The blind lead the blind. The taxi in front stops at a police checkpoint. We also draw to a halt. A dripping policeman shines a torch into our cab, is satisfied that my driver is correctly dressed, that I am not Mao Tse-tung, and on we dawdle.

Now we turn onto a road bordered by shallow canals that separate traffic from roadside houses. Most houses, other than those built on stilts, are connected to the road by flat wooden bridges. Sickly yellow reflections of window lights on the canals are pockmarked by rain.

The taxi in front is preparing to make a left-turn. It slows down, yellow indicator blinking, as the driver seeks the correct bridge. He turns off the road, misjudges the bridge and drives straight into the canal. As we pass I can see an illuminated cab like an island in the water. Partly submerged beams of light from the still functioning headlights highlight expanding ripples.

Idly, I wonder if anything under the bonnet drowned. The idea is not entirely fanciful. I remember a beautifully decorated jeep, ostensibly in excellent condition, that broke down at an altitude of 10,000 feet on an improbably narrow mountain road leading to Gilgit in north Pakistan. When the burly, turbanned driver lifted the bonnet to inspect the engine one immediately saw that everything, but everything, was held together by rotting rubber hoses, wires and coloured tapes. After tapping, hitting, knocking, pulling, twisting, slapping, punching and entreating various parts of the engine to no avail, the driver poked around behind the filth-encrusted battery where, completely enraged, he discovered a partly eaten and well chewed copy of the Koran, a nest of dead mice and two mouldy fried eggs.

My driver reacts to his colleague's misfortune by howling with laughter. He hoots, shakes his head, slaps his thighs and begins telling me how stupid some people are.

I only half listen. We have escaped traffic congestion but are still merely crawling along. To go any faster would be suicidal. The windscreen

is almost opaque with rain. The rain is heavy enough to reflect our headlights back against us. The waterlogged road, barely distinguishable from the bordering canals, is lit only by occasional headlight beams and lightning flashes. Houses are now very few and far between. No people can be seen. Palm trees bordering the canals are buffetted by the wind. The scene is unpleasantly reminiscent of the first five minutes of Hitchcock's *Psycho*.

The driver is telling me about the time his brakes failed on a winding mountain road in northern Thailand. He claims to have slowed the car by scraping it alongside a cliff face before switching off the ignition and letting the transmission brake the car.

He laughs at the memory before hastening to assure me that in fifteen years he has never had an accident caused by a driving error. No sooner are the words out of his mouth than there is a tortuously slow C-R-U-N-C-H. Impact. We are both thrown against the windscreen. Complete blackness. The engine splutters and dies.

A little shaken we both get out to discover that the taxi is inextricably embedded between the rear wheels of an unlit bulldozer parked at the side of the road. I am horrified. Had we have been travelling at speed. . .

As my driver throws a fit and inventively curses all past, present and future members of the municipality (and all their ancestors and offspring), I decide to walk home. There isn't really much choice. It is raining far too hard to wait for a taxi or bus. And the few travelling in this direction will be full by now, anyway.

I thrust money into the driver's hands and leave him to his emotional purification, magnificent insults and complaints about some people's stupidity screamed into the rain. Already soaked, I walk briskly, head lowered against the rain and wind. A few passing vehicles raise a fine film of spray to chill my legs. The journey is wet, lonely and dark. This is precisely one of those occasions when the very ordinary prospect of arriving home, showering, changing into dry clothes and enjoying a hot drink seems infinitely more appealing than attaining Nirvana or having a harem or enjoying champagne breakfasts everyday or owning a castle or retiring at the age of thirty.

Speculating on the comforts that await me at home, I am not fully aware of the sudden approach of a speeding bus. Momentarily I see it, crammed with steaming soaked passengers as it thunders past. For a few seconds it is like walking under a waterfall. A following truck re-drenches me. I am rapidly becoming disenchanted with twentieth-century mechanization.

A short-cut home is at hand. If I turn off the main road into a side street, walk through the courtyard of a Buddhist monastery, cross a wide canal by a high-arched footbridge, navigate a banana plantation, cross the railway branch line, brave dark (and snake-infested) orchards, I can arrive home quicker.

Deliberations. What have I to endure? At worst: the very real possibility of encountering snakes – cobras, banded kraits, vipers, pythons (and visiting sea snakes?); scorpions; centipedes; a dark, spooky Buddhist monastery courtyard (bats and maybe ghosts); pitch-black orchards (muddy at best, waterlogged at worst); I might get hit by a train; or be decapitated by a falling coconut; or fall into the canal (I can't swim).

Look, you want to see Hilary, don't you? Yes, but what about snakes, scorpions. . .? *Do you want to see Hilary or not?* Yes, but. . . *This way shortens the journey by twenty minutes, doesn't it?* Yes, but. . . *And it's probably your only chance of seeing him awake tonight.* Yes. *The answer's obvious then, isn't it?* Yes, I'll walk home the long way round.

At the corner of the side street, oh well, might as well try. Pass a dimly lit wooden noodle shop at the top of the street. Packed with dry, comfortable people drinking rice whisky, eating and laughing. They stare at me, the only pedestrian in sight – *walking without umbrella or raincoat in this weather!* – as though I am mad. Maybe I am.

The monastery courtyard is hauntingly beautiful as lightning casts dramatically large shadows of porcelain-studded pagodas onto the unlit chapel. I walk through the monks' quarters where a few weak lights indicate human presence. But I don't see a single person.

I arrive at the canal, still unhappy about the prospect of encountering snakes. Aaahh. First problems first. The bridge is treacherously slippery. The rain, if anything, is falling even harder now. Stumbling across the bridge, soaked to the skin, chilled to the bone, I am not in the happiest of moods. And then, several flashes of lightning and there below, etched in my mind forever, is a momentary image, an image typifying the Orient as perfectly as anything I have ever seen, an image as timeless as any sunrise or sunset, of an old Thai woman rowing home through the rain like a woman possessed.

It was worth a thousand soakings to have seen that.

Deep in the orchards there lived a taciturn old man who bred and trained fighting cocks. His stilted, single-roomed house, open to the sky, was so well concealed in a maze of coconut palms, banana, jackfruit and mango trees that people could walk within twenty yards of it and not see it. The house, made of grey unpainted wood long sucked dry by the tropical sun, was full of old yellowing photographs, calendars, Buddha images and well-thumbed, mildewed volumes on astrology; a few sticks of cane furniture occupied remaining space. Floorboards creaked underfoot and the entire house groaned, so much so that it forever seemed in danger of collapse but somehow the ancient timbers held together, almost as though bound by their unusual contents and an obstinacy inherited from their owner. At any time of the day the old man could be found in or about his house, sparring with young cocks – a gauntleted hand substituting as an opponent – exercising or grooming veterans, or sitting cross-legged in the deep shade of his verandah, contentedly puffing away at a bamboo water pipe and enjoying narcotic reveries. His wrinkled chest, back and arms were covered with fading tattoos – linear horoscopes and charms that appeared green on his chocolate-coloured skin.

Around the house more than twenty chickens and young cockerels would nonchalantly stroll, ignoring prize cocks roosting in individual cages. It mattered little to the old man whether he earned money or not. His food was brought to him daily by a niece who lived a ten-minute walk away. He rarely left his house for long. Visitors came to bargain for cockerels and aged cronies came to while away evenings drinking rice whisky. His expenditures must have been few. He had a tolerant affection for his animals, amusing but exasperating creatures at best, and contentedly adhered to an unvarying regimen day after day, week after week. So relaxed was his his life, it is doubtful if he bothered even to locate eggs laid by his own chickens in undergrowth surrounding his house.

Before Hilary's birth neither Anong nor I knew him very well. Sometimes we met him in the orchards and stopped to exchange pleasantries but never were we any more than passing acquaintances. It was, therefore, a total surprise when the old man came to our house one day and, to disguise, it seemed, extreme diffidence, brusquely offered us a chick for Hilary. Five-month-old son and old man regarded each other with uncertain smiles and the chick unsteadily explored its new house. Before long the old man softened and we were treated to a charming biography of said chick and given several hints on how to feed, groom and care for it.

Thereafter, the old man came to the house once or twice a week. He swapped tales with Anong – nonsense, delightfully recounted, like the cockerel that daily crowed at noon because it had been partly incubated by the midday sun, or blew our minds telling us about one of his great-grand-daughters who 'menstruates' with a monthly nosebleed – criticized (very sensibly) some of the drawings for this book, and cradled Hilary who, fascinated by the old man's tattoos, traced and pinched them with clumsy fingers. Son, old man and chick swiftly became firm friends.

Everything went well until the occurrence of one of those compounded disasters that life occasionally inflicts. One morning, quite unexpectedly, the old man's niece found him dead in bed. To our astonishment, he was eighty-three years old. And, that very same day, one of the mongrels scavenging in the orchards suddenly felt heroic and mauled Hilary's chick which died shortly afterwards. All in all, it was a complete pig of a day.

Spiders fascinate me.

I remember well a dilapidated sawmill worked mostly by aged men where a favourite pastime was to catch flies, earwigs and the occasional wasp and throw them into spiders' webs. The 'sport' took place in the men's rest-hut, a single long room, a filthy place into which strong sunlight could barely penetrate. The accumulated grime of several years was covered by sawdust and smoke-thickened cobwebs, thousands of which screened windows and hung like limp stalactites from the ceiling. Pieces of wood, yellowed newspapers, oily rags, wood shavings, logs, rusted saws, wire, grease and sweat-softened clothing and tools were piled against the walls. A fire-hazard, the hut was so dry it would have burned to ash within five minutes. Rats, wood lice, earwigs, spiders, flies – and seemingly every creeper and crawler that had ever existed – shared the hut with workmen.

During rest periods, after eating huge boiled-beef, pig's-liver, cheese, or fried-bacon-and-egg sandwiches, and guzzling pints of hot, sticky tea, the old men would catch insects and feed grotesquely obese spiders by flinging their catches into tunnel-like webs. Often there were bets, especially when the men were able to catch wasps. The size, weight, speed, age, defensive abilities (and probably the pedigree) of each web's occupant was common knowledge. A small spider versus an earwig, a wasp pitted against a large spider – the permutations were almost limitless. Odds were made and bets were placed. The unfortunate was thrown.

Invariably the bait would struggle. The spider would wobble out of its lair, smother the victim and drag the body into its larder. Sometimes an earwig made a perfunctory nip but the creature was doomed. Mostly, the spiders managed quick, unmessy operations. The only exception was when a wasp was able to sting a spider and send it hurrying back from whence it came, body palpitating and legs wildly out of synchronization. In such cases both stinger and stung perished. Like sadistic schoolboys the old men would cackle, bettors argue and obscenities be shouted across the hut. Arguments were resolved only when the time-whistle screeched and everyone unwillingly returned to work.

Late one morning, Anong excitedly shaking me awake. 'Come, come and look in the bathroom.' Half falling down the stairs, speculating on what mysteries will unfold in *John 1.* On the white tiled walls are hundreds of baby spiders. Mother, enormous, is on the floor, a punctured egg sac beside her. Hordes of the little buggers, a dozen would easily fit on a thumbnail, perfect replicas of the old lady, hesitantly moving in every direction. Wonder how many will survive. Chinchoks probably prepare ambushes already. During the day they slowly disperse, mother waiting until the last has reached the upper walls. Using the bathroom at night. Shaving. The sink is full of scummy water and beard particles. A straggler falls into the water. A sigh. About to perform a delicate rescue operation when the newlyborn does a Jesus Christ and streaks across the water, momentum carrying him up the

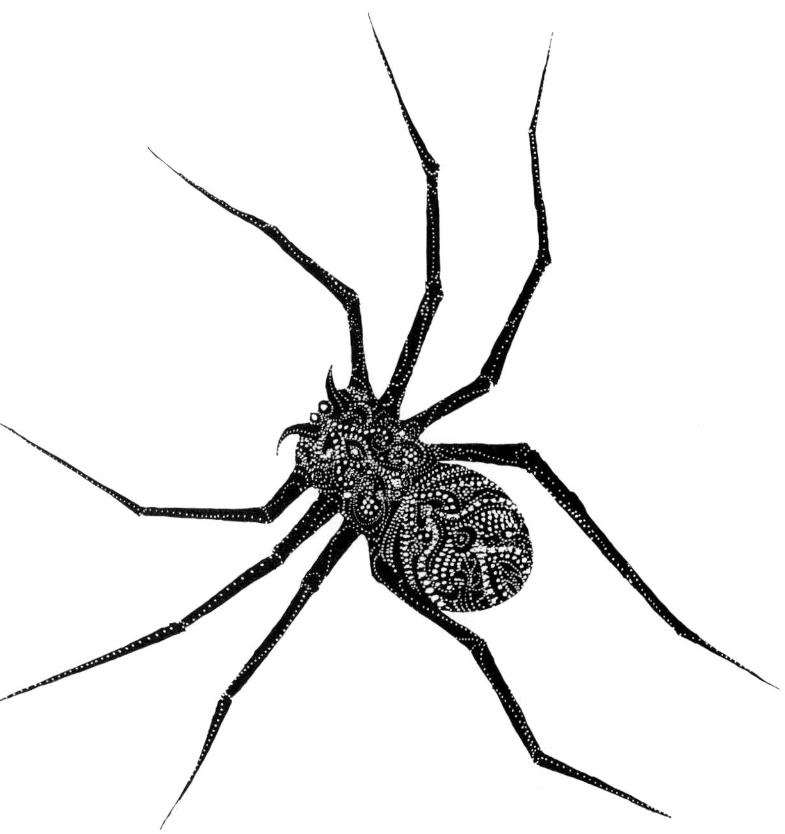

side of the sink to the top where he rests, exhausted, I imagine, by his biblical feat.

The early morning sight of other small ones resting in the centres of dewed webs – filagreed, perfect universes – resurrects the memory of a childhood tale in which thousands of spiders sang, danced and industriously worked through the night to make a lace gown for a beautiful girl, a memory belonging to days of tadpoles and newts in jam jars; of having a pocketful of pennies and feeling richer than Rockefeller; of collecting coveted tram tickets; comic books read under bed covers by torchlight; a buttered, crisp lettuce crammed between honey-dipped bread crusts; a beechwood discovered and explored in winter; wild strawberries and blackberries and plundering apple orchards and eating fresh, tart apples straight from the tree until the guts pleasantly ached; a plover's nest in a ploughed field, discovered after a three-day search; being thrown head over heels off the back of a galloping cow that didn't relish its role as a cavalry steed; making fires with twigs and dead leaves and roasting potatoes that were crisp black on the outsides and raw crisp on the insides; climbing hillside fir trees for panoramic views of 'enemy' territory; the first taste of beer, offered by an indulgent uncle; tobogganing down a steep slope, being catapulted into a deep drift and being nearly suffocated by wet, clammy snow – memories swiftly arriving at the frequent and surprising, yes surprising, because it is always fresh and marvellous, realisation, wow, I am a *father* and how good I feel, even a spider turns me on.

Sitting in the studio, morosely staring at the floor, a painting defiantly bad, mocking skills and artifices, bad, awful, terrible, the kind of day when it would be better to sleep under a palm tree, and then a tiny spider dances across the floor, a graceless *pas de huit,* a chinchok chuckles, the spider pirouettes and curtsies, I laugh, slap paint on the canvas and the day begins anew.

The sheer pleasure of taking Hilary for early morning walks! Carried, active, observant, a small dynamo doing original things like using freshly plucked flowers to clean his ears. Powdered, cool, fragrant, *sans* pants – his plumbing is so leaky – he notices orange-robed Buddhist monks collecting food from various houses and dogs sniffing long grass. Sunlight yellows tree tops but has yet to warm the cool earth. Spiders' webs crimple in soft breezes and householders yawn, throw open window shutters, scratch themselves, switch on radios and brew coffee. Houses are separated by trees, set back off paths, affording maximum privacy for everyone. Each house has its own compound and some are stockaded like pioneer forts.

We have a variety of routes to the same destination – an endlessly changing stream that runs among trees and under single plank bridges. Ducks waddle like dowager duchesses into the water, shiver, and allow the current to bear them away. Hilary stares with wide-eyed wonder at his first sight of swimming birds and makes appropriate noises. To amuse him I toss pebbles into the stream and we watch the widening ripples. Pleasing how a child's enthusiasm for simple things rubs off on the parents. Ripples rediscovered.

The young limping dog that always accompanies us ploughs through waist-high grass and inspects a toad slowly hopping towards the stream. The toad looks obscenely smug, reminding me of Sutherland's portrait of Somerset Maugham, and is unhurried, unfazed by the helping snout of the dog. For some reason the dog is called Fatty but he is slim, clumsy, has big floppy ears and a limp from puppyhood when a neighbour, smashed on whisky after an army reunion, grazed the dog with his car. Like many

cripples and afflicted persons, the dog is cheerful and good-natured. He has adopted us and that is that.

Gingerly crossing the stream, a single plank bending underfoot. A wooden, ramshackle coffee stall has opened and the owner's five naked children are noisily washing beside a rain-filled water jar. Opaque blocks of ice peek out from a pile of wet sawdust. Nearby, a gigantic rooster pecks the ground, brilliant wattles flapping and white body glistening. Black tail plumage is like a cascade of silk ribbons. Hilary makes noises and waves his hand at the rooster. I try to coax it nearer but, having seen so many cousins committed to the pot, the creature moves warily away. Fatty moves nearer to inspect the rooster which suddenly trots away like a surprised ostrich.

Walking through knee-high undergrowth on a narrow 'path'. Trees overhang and Hilary grabs leaves, showering us both with raindrops. Chuckle. And a red ant bites my neck. Chuckle.

On either side of the path trees cling to each other, overgrown, jungle-like. Wet undergrowth twists and curls around their trunks. Irrigation ditches are a mass of weeds and scum. One would need a machete to cut through.

We near the railway line, a straight surprisingly attractive path in an avenue of unrelieved green. Atop an incomplete wooden fence that guards nothing, a rust-coloured lizard is spastically moving. We stand and quietly watch. Fatty takes off, pursuing a low-flying butterfly. The lizard moves forwards, stops, long tail loosely hanging. It turns and stares at us. Impasse. And then we hear a train whistle and run the remaining distance to the track. A black wood-burning locomotive pulling a few shabby carriages rattles past. In a few hours it will cross the bridge on the River Kwai and head through the mountains towards the site of a recent millipede massacre. We wish it luck and return towards the house.

The lizard on the fence hasn't moved. In the distance the train whistle blows; the lizard remains motionless; Fatty reappears smacking his lips; and Hilary empties his bladder. On me. A less than leisurely return past the coffee stall where a few customers are breakfasting. We acknowledge greetings and walk towards the house with the owner's children who are lugging briefcases and bulging satchels to school. Practising their English alphabet, whooping, and I'm beginning to feel like a cross between a pied piper and Fagin. Incessant chatter and laughter, a little girl jumping up and down and tugging Hilary's shirt. He grins and moans, twists this way and that, chuckles, emits a long crackle of dirty laughter, looks miserable when the children wave goodbye and take another path to the main road.

Back to the house, past a small dwelling where a young girl is crooning as she washes clothes, stopping to exchange greetings with a friend and Anong comes to meet us. Transfer Hilary who claps his hands and, democratically, soaks his mother. Three happy, soaked people and a limping dog return home for breakfast.

Epilogue

There were many things that didn't quite make it: occurrences and sights like squirrels that leap on to and across the roof at unexpected moments; the evening a neighbour was bitten by a 'non-poisonous' snake and very nearly died; beetles helplessly lost between window screens and shutters like strangers in a foreign country; a strange dog proudly depositing a barely living rat at our feet in thanks for bones and waste food; millipedes making love in a plastic chamber pot; the sun-fermented perfume of the orchards after rainfall; a black lizard sunbathing on the balcony; Hilary attempting to befriend a paranoiac toad; bees drunkenly attempting to extract pollen from paint tubes; midday when dogs pant in the shade, birdsong ceases and the orchards slide into siesta; earwigs slinking across the verandah; the bat that entered the studio at night, circuited twice and noiselessly flapped away; red ants on the rampage; inquisitive black goats belonging to an Indian Moslem joyfully trotting among coconut palms like Arabs in an oasis; the afternoon an itinerant vendor lifted oranges from her pannier, exposing a gigantic asterisk of a spider that jerkingly ran into the house by the front door and, pursued, left by the back; monstrous snails winding through grass like an armoured column stealthily preparing for a dawn attack; a grasshopper suspiciously investigating an uncommunicative stick insect; a wasp building a miniature mud hut on a window shutter and sub-letting it to ants; mice that nested in the broken soundbox of a mandolin and who frequently played chords as they left on scavenging trips.

In another vein there might have been mention of the white peacocks nesting in the living room chandelier; of domestic strife when the butler discovered Hilary's rabbits chewing caviar in the pantry and Anong's pet leopard in the wine cellar; or of the house tokay that has learnt to whistle the Thai national anthem – one of our neighbours tried to claim damages from us, claiming his multiple ruptures are a direct result of having to suddenly stand to attention when carrying his refrigerator upstairs.

Anyway, this is: it. Hilary is a year old, and to the delight of us both, Anong is pregnant again. We are both very happy.

I have only one wish. I hope our next child is not a gibbon.

Customarily, the author's biographical data appears here. You know the kind of thing -- '. . and Carruthers spent seven years contemplating his armpit on a Greek hillside before reorganizing the Tibetan navy. . . .' Etc, etc.

However, Kristiaan Inwood has declined to furnish any such data on the understandable grounds that he's probably divulged more than enough already. . . .